THEOPOLITAN READING

THEOPOLIS FUNDAMENTALS SERIES INTRODUCTION

The Theopolis Institute is a community of pastors, theologians, and students devoted to articulating and disseminating a vision of the church's mission to contemporary culture, a vision that centers on biblical theology and liturgical practice. The church carries on her world-transforming mission by being the church. When the church inhabits the symbolic world of the Bible through the liturgy, and communes together at the Lord's table, she becomes a source of light and life to the world.

Theopolis teaches, develops tools, and fosters networks to assist church leaders throughout the world to form thoroughly biblical, liturgical, and catholic churches. The Theopolis Institute is not a church, but is like scaffolding to assist the church in rebuilding God's heavenly city so that it can effectively carry out her mission of transforming the cities of man.

The Theopolis Institute was established in 2013, but its leaders have been working together to formulate and teach a Theopolitan vision of Bible, liturgy, church, and culture for several decades through James B. Jordan's Biblical Horizons.

The Theopolis Fundamentals Series introduces the Biblical Horizons / Theopolis outlook and agenda to a new generation. The early volumes of the series summarize our convictions about biblical interpretation, liturgical theology and practice, and the church's cultural and political mission. The Fundamentals will be followed by a collection of Theopolis Explorations volumes that will examine Scripture, liturgy, and culture in more depth and detail.

For more information about Theopolis, visit our web site at TheopolisInstitute.com.

THEOPOLITAN READING

PETER J. LEITHART
PHD, UNIVERSITY OF CAMBRIDGE
PRESIDENT OF THEOPOLIS INSTITUTE

BOOKS
AN IMPRINT OF ATHANASIUS PRESS

Theopolitan Reading
by Peter J. Leithart

Theopolis Books

Copyright © 2020 Theopolis Books
An Imprint of Athanasius Press

Athanasius Press
715 Cypress Street
West Monroe, Louisiana 71291
www.athanasiuspress.org

Cover design: Ryan Harrison
Typesetting: Christopher D. Kou

ISBN: 978-1-7351690-0-2

All rights reserved. No part of this publication may be reproduced, stored in a retrieval system, or transmitted in any form or by any means—electronic, mechanical, photocopy, recording, or any other—except for brief quotations in printed reviews, without the prior permission of the publisher.

Throughout this book, the author has frequently referred to passages from the New American Standard Bible (NASB) published by the Lockman Foundation. Since the NASB passages quoted represent a minimal part of the original document, it constitutes fair use. All other Bible passages were translated by Peter J. Leithart and are reproduced without any further alterations from Hebrew and Greek texts, which are in the public domain.

CONTENTS

Acknowledgements	vii
Blessed City	ix
To the Reader	xi
Chapter 1 Spiritual Reading	001
Chapter 2 World	025
Chapter 3 Adam	051
Chapter 4 Eve	073
Chapter 5 Eden	091
Epilogue	111
For Further Reading	115

ACKNOWLEDGEMENTS

A number of friends and colleagues contributed to the production of *Theopolitan Reading*. I am grateful to Jeff Meyers and Alastair Roberts for reading through the manuscript and offering their comments. Ashton Moats and John Barach proofread the book and saved me from many errors of spelling, grammar, citation, and detail. Thanks to Chris Kou for typesetting the book, and to Jarrod Richey of Athanasius Press for overseeing the publication process.

BLESSED CITY

1. Blessed city, heavenly Salem,
   vision dear of peace and love,
   who of living stones art builded
   in the height of heaven above,
   and with angel hosts encircled,
   as a bride dost earthward move!

2. From celestial realms descending,
   bridal glory round thee shed,
   meet for him whose love espoused thee,
   to thy Lord shalt thou be led;
   all thy streets and all thy bulwarks
   of pure gold are fashioned.

3. Bright thy gates of pearl are shining,
   they are open evermore;
   and by virtue of his merits
   thither faithful souls do soar,
   who for Christ's dear name in this world
   pain and tribulation bore.

4 Many a blow and biting sculpture
　polished well those stones elect,
　in their places now compacted
　by the heavenly Architect,
　who therewith hath willed for ever
　that his palace should be decked.

5 To this temple, where we call thee,
　come, O Lord of Hosts, to-day;
　with thy wonted loving-kindness
　hear thy servants as they pray,
　and thy fullest benediction
　shed within its walls alway.

6 Here vouchsafe to all thy servants
　what they ask of thee to gain,
　what they gain from thee for ever
　with the blessed to retain,
　and hereafter in thy glory
　evermore with thee to reign.

7 Laud and honour to the Father,
　laud and honour to the Son,
　laud and honour to the Spirit,
　ever Three, and ever One,
　consubstantial, co-eternal,
　while unending ages run.

JOHN MASON NEALE

TO THE READER

*Solid food is for the mature, who because of practice
have their senses trained
to discern good and evil.*
Hebrews 5:14

May I quote myself? Well, you can't stop me, so I'll go ahead. In *The Theopolitan Vision*, I wrote,

> Authority is *always* exercised through words. Honoring authority means honoring the words that authorities speak. If we bow to the authority of God the Lord, then we bow to the authority of His Word. His Word is the ultimate Word, bearing ultimate authority. If anything contradicts the Lord's Word, it must be false. Every other authority has to submit to the authority of the Word of God.

I also wrote,

> There is nothing in human life outside the authority of Scripture. If Jesus is Lord of all, He governs *all* by His Word. That means there is no space that's safe from a turf war between Jesus and other authorities. Scripture challenges the status

quo, calling for repentance, calling us to die and rise. If Jesus is Lord of all, there are no Scripture-free zones.

As Cornelius Van Til liked to say, scripture is authoritative on everything about which it speaks, and it speaks about *everything*.

We can't leave it at that, though. We need to ponder how Scripture speaks to everything. We might hope it works something like this:

- Theo has a decision to make.
- Theo consults the Bible.
- The Bible tells Theo what decision to make.

For some questions, the Bible functions just like that:

- Theo is trying to decide whether or not to start an affair with his secretary.
- Theo consults the Bible and finds Exodus 20.
- The Bible tells Theo, "*No!*"

Everyone knows the Bible doesn't work like that for everything. It can't.

- Theo is trying to choose between two different job offers.
- Theo consults the Bible and finds nothing.
- Theo takes the job with the highest salary.

After that, Theo puts his Bible on the shelf and never looks at it again on a weekday.

When people discover the Bible doesn't *directly and specifically* address every question they ask or every dilemma they face, they might decide to dispense with Scripture or at least relegate it to a secondary status. The Bible gives spiritual direction, but when it comes to real life, we need "wisdom" or "natural law," not the Bible. The Bible isn't detailed enough to be practical, and, besides, it's awfully vague.

TO THE READER

That response is just another version of Theo's decision to store his Bible. If Theo is looking for something on the order of, "Thou shalt take the HVAC job," it's not surprising he can't find what he is looking for. But that doesn't mean the Bible has nothing to say. Indulge me while I quote myself again:

> The Bible doesn't tell us how to build a widget, but it tells us a lot that informs our widget-building. It tells us *why* we labor, teaches us to devote our widget-building energies to serving our neighbor, commands us to be honest in our widget-building, requires us to love the widget-builders beside or under us. Sometimes the Bible's instruction is very general: Whatever you do, whether you eat or drink, do all to the glory of God (1 Cor 10:31). Sometimes, it's very specific: If someone slaps you on the right cheek, turn the other cheek (Matt 5:39). General or specific or somewhere between, Scripture speaks to all people in every circumstance.

Scripture is our final and highest authority for *everything*, in all circumstances. Scripture doesn't give you a shortcut. We can't avoid the tough work of sorting out the issues. We need to give thoughtful consideration to facts. We need to ask advice. We need to pay attention to our desires, the circumstances of our lives, the good of our community and church, and on and on. Scripture commands or encourages all of these efforts. God doesn't speak to my life in a way that bypasses *me*.

Yet, even when we get advice from the wise (which we should) or examine the facts (which we can't avoid), we still run the advice and our interpretation of the facts through the sifter of Scripture. All through the process, we're engaged with Scripture. There's no Bible-free zone. There's no Bible-free moment. All the time, in all circumstances, we answer to the Word of God. We're always saying, "Yes," or "No," to the Bible.

Theo made a key mistake. Many Christians do. Scripture isn't written mainly to answer my questions or make my decisions. It's not primarily addressed to my circumstances or dilemmas. It's addressed to *me*. Through His Word, God transforms *me* into a living image of the living Word. He remakes us so we can remake the world according to the pattern of Scripture. He trains our senses to know good and evil.

That includes *moral* formation. Scripture teaches us what is good and evil. It includes *intellectual* formation. It teaches us what is true and false. We forget that Scripture also forms our *imaginations*. And we forget that a Scripturally-shaped imagination is essential to moral and intellectual formation and action.

We face a moral choice, which seems to present clear-cut options: X or Y. Join the militant first-century Zealots or just keep your head down and look away? It takes imagination to see another option: "Turn the other cheek. Give your cloak. Go the second mile." Jesus teaches neither revolution nor quietism but martyrdom, *resistant* witness.

You're faced with an intellectual puzzle: Apples fall. Planets stay in their orbits. Perhaps—Sir Isaac says in a blaze of insight—perhaps these are two manifestations of the *same* force. Modern physics rests on an *imaginative* leap that was later demonstrated by mathematics and experimentation.

You're faced with a political dilemma: When a novel virus begins to spread throughout the world, should you shut down schools, businesses, and churches? Or should you control the spread and wait it out? Especially when all the pressure in the world pushes you to move in one direction or another, it takes an extraordinarily imaginative leader to find an alternative route.

We make moral and intellectual breakthroughs when we learn to see the world anew.

That's what the Bible does. It targets our hearts, minds, senses, emotions, and imaginations to form *us* so we engage the world with a well-stocked, that is, a *biblically*-stocked

TO THE READER

imagination. If you submit to what you hear in the Word, it transforms the way you see, the way you take hold of things, your ability to sniff out problems and unexpected solutions, your taste for defeat and delight. Scripture applies to everything because it applies to all of *you*. It gives you new ears and eyes and hands, a new nose and tongue.

We never leave it behind or move it to the background. We always consult it with specific questions because we never know ahead of time if it will give us a specific answer. But we don't consult it periodically when we have a tough choice. We maintain a steady diet of Scripture because over time the Spirit uses the Word to train our bodies to do justice. Through the Spirit, the Word matures us to become kings and queens, prepared for every good work. If *Theopolitan Reading* awakens your imagination, even for a moment, I will have accomplished my purpose.

But we still can't leave it at that. We need to ask *how* Scripture speaks, how it rouses our imaginations. We have to ask which "method" of interpretation we should follow. We have to discuss hermeneutics, the theory of interpretation. That's what this little book is about.

What should we call what we at Theopolis do when we read the Bible? What should we call "our hermeneutics"? How best to describe "Theopolitan reading"? It's not easy to locate Theopolis on the hermeneutical map. We don't quite fit anywhere.

We happily stand with Fundamentalists who believe the Bible is true in the everyday sense of "true." The days of creation were normal days, Balaam's donkey spoke, Jesus raised Lazarus and multiplied loaves and fish. We love Fundamentalists so much that we called this series the "Theopolis Fundamentals." Unfortunately, Fundamentalists won't have us. Unlike most Fundamentalists, we're *not* "literalists." We're positively giddy about the symbolic dimensions of Scripture.

We admire premodern interpretation, but we're too Protestant to be allegorists. Like allegorists, we're convinced that every detail matters, no matter how minute. The Spirit speaks in all these details, and He doesn't waste His breath. We love unraveling puzzles: Why is the heifer red (Num 19:2)? Why does Scripture record the number of baskets of leftovers after Jesus fed the multitudes (Matt 14:20; 15:37)? We assume these numbers mean something, but *what?* Why did John say the disciples caught 153 fish (John 21:11)? Scripture leaves out a lot of details. Biblical writers are reticent. We always need to ask *why* they include what they do include. There's always a reason, and the details always edify. It's the glory of God to conceal a matter, and He's hidden a lot of treasure in the pages of Scripture. He does that to train us to be kings, whose glory is to uncover secret things (Prov 25:2).

Unlike many allegorists, though, we don't translate the Bible into some moral or philosophical idiom. We don't move from "body" to "soul," from "letter" to "spirit," or from this world to heaven. That shift betrays the nature-supernatural dichotomy I railed against in *The Theopolitan Vision*. We renounce allegory of that sort, with all its pomp and show. We're too enamored of the letter to be comfortable among allegorists. We do pretty much the opposite. We want Scripture to judge and refine every language and system. We read the Bible on its own terms and don't allow some other ideology to set the terms for Scripture. We don't translate the Bible into a worldly language. We translate the world into Biblese.

If "typology" refers to a theology of history, what we do counts as typology. That's not what most people mean by "typology." They usually mean the habit of digging through Scripture for snippets and snapshots of Jesus. We agree Scripture is filled with snapshots and shadows, but it's more complex than that. We're alert to internal analogies (e.g., Saul is a new Gideon, Sarah a new Eve, Sinai a new Eden), and we complain when someone "jumps to Jesus" before exploring the immediate historical and literary context in depth.

Besides, the Old Testament doesn't just foreshadow Jesus. It foreshadows what Augustine called the "whole Christ," head-and-body, Jesus and the church. Adam is a type of Christ, but Eve is a type of the church (Eph 6:22-33). Moses is a type of Jesus, but Moses is head of Israel. The exodus is a type of salvation—specifically, a type of baptism and Eucharist (1 Cor 10:1-5). When you begin to catch the scent of the body of Christ within types of Christ, you can find yourself within the typologies of the Bible. The whole Bible is about Christ, but He is head of His body, so it's all about the church. The whole Bible is about Christ, but you are a member of His body, so it's all about *you*. The whole Bible is about Christ, but the Eucharist is His body and blood, so the whole Bible is about the bath and the table. Typology expands to encompass the cosmos: The whole Bible is about Christ, but Jesus is the new Adam who reigns over and fills all things. The Bible is about Christ, but *all things* cohere in Him. The Bible is about Christ, and *just for that reason*, it's about everything. If that's what you mean by "typology," then, sure, we do typology.

There are other possibilities. We might call what we do "biblical theology" or "redemptive-historical," but everybody uses those terms. They don't capture the distinctiveness of Theopolitan reading and teaching. We might call it "literary" reading, and there's something to that. We've learned a lot from literary studies of the Bible, but we get queasy when literary readers rely on categories of modern criticism (like "genre"). And we're too concerned with politics—with the import of the text for the real world—to stop at literary analysis. We agree with John Frame: Theology *is* application. It's gotta preach.

Years ago, Jim Jordan criticized the "interpretive minimalism" of biblical studies, and someone decided he must favor

THEOPOLITAN READING

"interpretive maximalism." That's a misleading label. We *do* want to hear everything God speaks, and we think everything He says means something. But reading isn't a game where the reader with the most connections wins.

We might call it "symbolic interpretation." That's accurate enough, and important. The loss of the symbolic imagination is one of the diseases of modernity, and it infects the church. Theopolis aims to renew Christian imagination by cultivating Scriptural imagination. But we reject symbolic or mythical readings that deny the Bible's historicity. Besides, we don't treat the Bible as a code where every **X** (water, fire, tree) stands directly and necessarily for some **Y** (baptism, sacrifice, the cross). We're too attuned to the immediate context, too enamored of the letter, for that.

Our method looks a lot like the medieval Quadriga, which explored the "fourfold sense" of Scripture. According to this model, every passage of Scripture tells us what happened (literal), what to believe (allegorical), what to do (tropological), and what to hope for (anagogical). Every passage reports on real people and events, points to Christ, guides our lives, projects us toward a glorious future. But "Quadriga" is unfamiliar, and it's even weirder when we turn it into an adjective. Trust me, you can't use "Quadrigal Hermeneutics" in a fund-raising letter.

At bottom, we're skeptical of hermeneutical "method" in general. Methods pre-determine what questions get asked and what answers count. Reading is artful. It's not a mechanistic process where inputs chug out predictable outcomes. Hermeneutical method often implies that the ideal reader is a lone scholar in his study, rather than a worshiper in a liturgical assembly. Methods can make us forget the role of mentors and conversation partners. Armed with a method, the reader reads to master the text when he's supposed to be mastered by it.

There's no substitute for soaking in Scripture, reading it again

TO THE READER

and again and again, until it's in our bones and blood. There's no substitute for mentors and models who train you to read. There's no substitute for being in a church where Scripture is read, sung, chanted, prayed, preached, taught. There's no substitute for a thorough, weekly liturgical basting in Scripture. Theopolitan reading is inseparable from the dialogue of Theopolitan liturgy.

In the end, I'm ready to throw in the towel on this exercise in naming. It looks as if we'll have to take our own place on the map. Let's just call it a "Theopolitan reading," and there, an end.

One last introductory comment, and we'll be off. You might have picked up this book because you want to learn to read the Bible better. A book will help. Hopefully, *this* book will help. But this book won't help by giving you rules and procedures. To read well, you don't need a set of rules. What you need are models, mentors, and teachers who follow the reading of Jesus.

That's what I have to offer: *myself* as a mentor and model. I ask you, as Paul does, to imitate me insofar as I imitate Jesus, *the* Model Reader. If I am truly reading in the Spirit, following me will keep you in step with the Spirit. And then you will mature, with your senses trained to know good and evil.

1 SPIRITUAL READING

My ears you have opened.
Psalm 40:6

God speaks. He speaks the world into being (Gen 1). His speech sustains the swirling universe in its swirling. He speaks before there is anyone to hear or answer. He speaks to form those who hear and answer. He speaks in the last days in human flesh (John 1:1-4). He will speak again at the last day, sending many to everlasting glory and some to everlasting torment.

God speaks because God *is* Word—*eternally* Word. From forever and forever, unto ages of ages, whether or not the world ever is or was, the Father speaks the Word. And the Spirit (Heb. *ruach*; Gr. *pneuma*) is the energetic Breath of God, the Lord and Giver of life, who enlivens Father and Son and gives force to the Father's eternal Word.

God not only speaks but *writes*. He engraves Ten Words with His finger on the tablets of stone (Exod 31:18; Deut 9:10). He comes as Word to Abraham (Gen 15:4), Samuel (1 Sam 15:10), Nathan (2 Sam 7:4), Isaiah (Isa 38:4), and He comes as Word to inspire prophets to write words (Jer 30:2; Ezek 1:3; 3:4-6; Hos 1:1; 4:1).

Even in the new covenant, when the covenant of the "letter" has given way to the covenant of Spirit, Paul spends his career writing epistles, and John is repeatedly told to "write" what he sees and hears (Rev 1:11, 19; 2:1; 3:1; 14:13; 19:9; 21:5). Words on parchment make the Corinthians into a living epistle, Paul's corporate "letter of recommendation" (2 Cor 3:1-7). By Paul's words, they receive the Word of God, solid food to make them mature.

"Jesus never wrote anything," you'll often hear from Christians who want to minimize the centrality of the Bible in the life of the church. *Au contraire!* As the Word, He's been writing since He met Moses on Mount Sinai.

Like the Word, the Spirit *writes*. He *is* God's Finger (compare Matt 2:28 with Luke 11:20), the Finger who does wonders beyond the skill of Egypt's magicians (Exod 8:19) and the Finger who writes on Sinai's stone tablets (Exod 31:18). The Word comes to the prophets, but the Spirit "carries" them to speak from God (2 Pet 1:21). The writings (Gr. *graphai*) are God-breathed, God's breath made text, "Spirited-out" (Gr. *theopneustos*) for our instruction (2 Tim 3:16-17).

That's who God is: Eternal Speaker, Eternal Word, Eternal Breath.

At the climax of the creation week, God forms man, male and female, and declares man is made in the image and likeness of God (Gen 1:26-28). What does that mean? An obvious way to answer that question is to answer these first: What has God been doing? What is God *like*?

We learn a lot about God from Genesis 1, but one thing stands out: God speaks. If we're made in the image of this God, we must be speaking beings—creatures who communicate in unique ways with the Creator, creatures with ears to hear the Creator's voice, creatures who share the Creator's power to make-by-speaking, creatures who speak and write and feast on the Creator's Word.

Adam becomes a living soul by the "breath" of God (Gen 2:7). The Hebrew word for "soul" (*nephesh*) derives from a verb (*naphash*) that means "to take a breath." Adam is given breath so he can speak back to the speaking God.

Breath gives our spoken words force. Without breath, we couldn't speak at all. Spoken words *are* articulated breath. We control airflow to form meaningful sounds—"o" rather than "a," "p" rather than "c," "pin" rather than "sin." Our breath gives rhetorical force to what we speak. We decrease or increase the volume, speak in staccato or legato, raise or lower the pitch. We are speaking beings because we are "living souls" who live by the Breath of God.

As the Father speaks His eternal Word by the power of His eternal Breath, so we His creatures speak by the power of breath.

Christians are sometimes puzzled by the very existence of the Bible. How can a God who is Spirit communicate through physical means: markings on a page or vibrations in the air? Why *would* He? Surely God must speak in a more refined, less crassly material fashion.

That's not how the God revealed in Scripture works. He speaks in human language, taking time to speak to us. It takes time to hear and read His Word. Our bodies are involved as we train our eyes and ears. All human learning takes place through language, which means that all language engages our bodies and affirms the goodness of time and space and all created things. The Creator speaks to His creatures through His creation.

The Bible—the physical book made of nothing but ink on paper—is the product of the Father's speaking by Word and Spirit. Scripture is God's words in human words because our God is omnilingual, a Speaker of every human tongue.

To read such a text well, we need to read in step with the Word and Spirit who are the Author of the text. Right reading of a Spirit-inspired book must be Spiritual reading.

THEOPOLITAN READING

Models and Mentors

How did you learn to speak? Did your parents lock you in isolation for a year or two until you gained linguistic competence? Were you alone as you prepared to unleash yourself on other speakers? If so, congratulations! You're the first of your kind.

We may have a biological or genetic predisposition toward language. But we learn actual languages by being spoken to and by learning to speak back. We learn to speak in communion. Our drive to speak arises from a desire for communion. Speech deepens and sustains communion. Conversation is the ground in which our created capacity for language becomes fruitful. As in God, Word and Breath are the bond of our communion.

How did you learn to *read*? Were you locked in your first-grade cubicle and sternly warned not to come out until you were ready? Probably not, unless Dickens's Mr. M'Choakumchild was your primary school teacher. You learned to read the way you learned to speak—through parents who read to you and teachers who taught you to recognize letters and to string letters into words and words into sentences, paragraphs, and books.

You learned to read because you had models and mentors—people who showed you how to read by reading, people who peered over your shoulder to guide your reading, to correct misreading, and to commend your right readings.

We learn to read *well* in the same way. You don't become an intelligent or insightful reader in an isolation chamber. Textbooks and rules can help, but books can't teach everything you need to learn. Sometimes rulebooks are counter-productive since they can seduce you into thinking reading is a mechanical process: Stuff the right ingredients in one end, and sausage will come out the other.

To read well, you need models and mentors. You need to watch or read or hear people reading well and learn to mimic them. You need a mature reader standing beside your shoulder to tell you what you're doing right and what you're doing wrong, until you learn to hear with his ears and see with his eyes.

Spiritual reading is reading guided by the Spirit of God. We discern the Author's full intent by being filled with the Author Himself. When Christ the Word dwells in us, we receive the written word rightly. The Spirit is our Mentor.

Above all, the Spirit teaches us to read by pointing us to the Model Reader, Jesus. Spiritual reading means reading as Jesus read.

As the Word anointed by the Spirit beyond measure, He is the Model Reader of the law. According to Jesus' reading, the Torah is focused on justice, mercy, and truth (Matt 23:23). According to Jesus, keeping the law is identical to following Him (Matt 5—7).

Jesus comes to "fulfill" the law (Matt 5:17-19) in the first instance by doing justice in His own life. Jesus shows what the First Word requires by loving and obeying His Father above all things, even at the cost of His life. He wars against hypocrites, against the practical idolatry prohibited in the Third Word. By healing on the Sabbath, He gives Sabbath to the weary and heavy-laden. He doesn't merely refrain from killing but offers Himself up to murderers. He doesn't merely refrain from theft but pays debts He doesn't owe—our debts. He is the faithful witness even though His true witness leads to a Roman cross. His entire life is a "reading" of the Torah.

Jews categorize a large portion of the Hebrew Bible as "prophecy." They view the books Christians usually call "historical books" as "former prophets," while what we call "prophecy" they consider "latter prophets." By His teaching and life, the Spirit-anointed Jesus is the Model Reader of prophecy just as He's the Model Reader of the law.

Jesus is literally another "Joshua," sharing the name of the conqueror of Canaan and carrying Joshua's war against

THEOPOLITAN READING

idols at a deeper level. Clothed with the Spirit, Jesus is another Gideon or Samson. He's the "son of David," a King greater than Solomon (Matt 12:42). His body is a temple, ruined like Solomon's but rebuilt as in the days of Joshua and Zerubbabel (John 2:13-20). He fulfills Hosea 11:1 by escaping from a Pharaoh-like king of the Jews (Matt 2:14-15). He's Isaiah's Spirit-filled Servant (Luke 4:16-21), a greater Elijah who feeds outcast widows (Luke 4:25-26), and a greater Elisha who cleanses Gentile lepers (Luke 4:27). Jesus is the key to Israel's history and prophecy.

Jesus sums it all up when He appears to the disciples after His resurrection. On the road to Emmaus, He's appalled that the two disciples don't understand that the Christ had to suffer and die and be raised. Beginning with Moses and moving through all the prophets, He tells them "in all the Scriptures the things concerning Himself" (Luke 24:27; cf. 24:44-49).

Even after they walk with Jesus from Jerusalem to Emmaus, even after they feel their hearts burning in them, even after Jesus teaches them about the Christ from all the Scripture, the two disciples *still* don't recognize Him. Jesus is the Model Reader, but even that isn't enough.

The disciples recognize Jesus is with them *only* when Jesus gives thanks and breaks bread. *Then* their eyes are open. Jesus the Model Reader is also Jesus the Host and table companion (Luke 24:30-31). Bible and liturgy can't be separated.[1] Scripture needs to be before our eyes, ringing in our ears, and tasted on our tongues. Within the liturgy, Scripture trains our senses so we can receive the solid food of Scripture so we become ever more mature. We learn to read well when we break bread with the Master.

You might be looking for an out: "OK, Jesus is the Model Reader, but I can learn to read from Jesus without any help from

---

[1] For more, see *Theopolitan Liturgy*, ch. 2.

any other human beings. I've got the Spirit and Jesus and the book. What else do I need?"

Protestants are apt to be seduced by this line of thought. We confess the "perspicuity" of Scripture, its clarity. We stress the priesthood of all believers and believe each believer has access to God. It seems reasonable to conclude that the Spirit gives us insight into the Word He inspired. Each of us can sit in his cell and learn to read. Sure, when we learn the *natural* process of reading, we need teachers. But when it comes to supernatural, *Spiritual* reading, we can dispense with models, mentors and teachers.

True, the Spirit *is* our teacher. He's the Finger by which Jesus bores open our deaf ears so we can hear what He has to say (Mark 7:33). But it's an error to conclude that the Spirit bypasses teachers, our bodies, and time. The Spirit guides us through *means*. We mature as we become more like our mentors and models.

It's always been so. The ascended Jesus gives gifts to the church, including teachers and pastors (Eph 4:7-16). The Spirit of Jesus equips those who teach with the ability to edify the church in their teaching (Rom 12:3-8; 1 Cor 12:4-11). You can't be in step with the Spirit if you reject the Spirit's gifts. You can't be a Spiritual reader without learning from Spirit-filled teachers (cf. Acts 8:1).

Jesus is *the* model Reader, but the New Testament is the work of *many* Spirit-filled model readers. Matthew, Mark, Luke, and John paint the life of Jesus from the palette of the Old Testament. The Gospels teach how the events, characters, and institutions of Scripture come to fulfillment in the Christ.

Paul teaches that Jesus is the new Adam (Rom 5:12-21), the Spiritual son of Abraham (Gal 3:1-14; 4:21-31), the seed of David (Rom 1:1-4). The writer to the Hebrews says Jesus' blood speaks a better word than the blood of Abel (Heb 12:24) and that Jesus is a priest after the order of Melchizedek, surpassing the order of Aaron (Heb 7). Jesus' death, resurrection, and ascent fulfill the sacrifices of the Mosaic order (Heb 9—10). And so on and on and still on. The apostles learned well from the Model Reader and teach the Scriptures just as He taught.

Jesus still models reading by giving us model readers. The Scriptures are clear, written for every follower of Jesus. That doesn't mean they are equally clear to everyone. It doesn't mean the Scriptures are clear in the absence of teachers to clarify. Scripture is clear because the Spirit guides our reading by giving us guides.

Protestants often transpose "priesthood of all believers" into a democratic tune or an egalitarian etude. Because we're all priests, we think we all have equal skill in reading, teaching, grasping texts.

That's an error. Some men and women are more "naturally" gifted to understand texts. Some have devoted focused energy and enormous time to learning how to read well. Some have drunk the milk, trained their senses, and learned to eat solid food. Such mature readers are *better* readers than the rest of us. The best thing you can do is recognize their superiority and put yourself under their tutelage, imitating them as they imitate Christ.

Think about rules for reading as an instruction manual for car repair. If you're a beginner, you need the manual. You may have to follow the instructions quite strictly: Remove *this* bolt, replace *this* washer, turn the oil filter *that* direction, and never NEVER! remove this hose when the engine is hot. As long as you're following the manual, you're not a good mechanic. Good mechanics *know* engines. They can diagnose by listening to the clicks and clacks coming from under the hood. You become a good mechanic by apprenticeship to a car guy. He embodies the rules, and you infer the rules of the game from watching him work. Or, even better, you imitate the master mechanic until the feel for good

SPIRITUAL READING

practices seeps into your body and bones.

Rulebooks can't enforce the rules. They can't alert you to violations. *Experience* alerts you to violations. The car will let you know. You'll know you removed the wrong hose when some slick, boiling fluid starts spewing from the engine. You remember the rule: "Never NEVER! remove that hose when the engine is hot." You can avoid mistakes and injury if you stick close to the master mechanic. He'll tell you if you start to do something dumb.

Whether we're repairing a car, playing an instrument, swinging a bat, tossing a free throw, or reading, the pattern is the same. A rulebook may contain standards of judgment, but a rulebook can't *judge*. Mature people, with senses trained to discern good and evil, teach us what to do and what not to do. *Other people* provide the brakes and checks that keep our reading on track and keep us from driving over a cliff. As you practice and listen to your mentor, you'll develop guidelines and rules. But they come later. Rules don't come first. Rules always come *after* a practice has begun.

For centuries, the church accepted Jesus and the apostles as model readers, learning to read the Scriptures, *and everything else*, by following their example and instruction. Teachers of the past weren't always good readers. They got things wrong. But their "method" was sound because they read in the Spirit.

For the past several centuries, that "method" has been mocked, even by many Christians. Modern "scientific" hermeneutics promises to teach us to read more accurately. It teaches us to reject childish "allegorization" and to pay close attention to the grammar and historical context so we can discern the hard facts of the case. Modern hermeneutics trains us to take fright at the "eisegesis" of the church's reading, its alleged habit of reading Jesus into the Bible instead of following the literal lineaments of the text.

Modern scholarship has made immeasurable contributions

THEOPOLITAN READING

to our knowledge of the Bible. We know far more about the ancient contexts of the Hebrew Bible and New Testament than any previous age of church history. We have made great strides in grasping the languages of the ancient world. Archeological discoveries like the Dead Sea Scrolls have opened up forgotten features of the biblical world.

Plus, the church has *always* insisted on attention to the letter of Scripture, the grammar of the text, and its historical setting. Spiritual reading assumes the persons and events recorded in Scripture occurred in real time and space. Unless they are real, we are of all men most miserable. Modern scholars remind us to take the literal sense very seriously. To that degree, they, too, are gifts of the Spirit who model good reading. We take those warnings to heart and affirm the Reformers' correct insistence on the priority of the letter. The Spiritual reading I model here doesn't leave the letter behind. It plumbs the depths of the letter, which, we discover, opens out into glimpses of Jesus, frameworks for understanding the world. We seek to understand the text on the terms it sets for us. By the Spirit, the letter trains our senses to discern between good and evil.

At a fundamental level, though, modern biblical scholarship is a systematic, relentless, centuries-long experiment in quenching the Spirit. It replaces Jesus as Model Reader with a scientific, grammatical, or historical master. The Word is our food. It trains our senses and makes us mature. If we want to put away childish things, nothing is more crucial to the future of the church than repentance at this point. We must turn to get back in step with the Spirit, learning to read well by imitating the model reading of Jesus and His apostles.

SPIRITUAL READING

Reading Well

Modern criticism of Jesus' way of reading hits home. Jesus seems to read the Hebrew Scriptures arbitrarily, and so do the other writers of the New Testament. *Are* they good readers or sloppy readers? Do they see what's in the text, or are they making things up? What, after all, does "reading well" mean?

Reading well doesn't simply mean understanding the words and sentences. Reading well isn't the ability to repeat what you've read. Everyone who is competent in a language can repeat what he reads. A *good* reader understands exactly what the text communicates, and he seeks to understand everything the text communicates. A good reader strives to understand accurately *and* fully, without sacrificing either to the other.

Or we might put it this way: A good reader hears the *poetry* of a text. We usually use "poem" and "poetry" to describe a particular kind of writing. Poems are written in lines and stanzas, have meter and rhyme, use devices like similes and metaphors and personification.

But all language has poetic features. The English word for "poem" comes from the Greek *poiema*, which simply means "a made thing." In this etymological sense, every text is "poetic" since it's built from the bricks and blocks and fasteners of language. Good readers notice everything about a text's construction.

Hard-headed realists bristle at nonsense like "my love is like a red, red rose" or "hope is a thing with feathers" or "shall I compare thee to a summer's day?" I'd rather you wouldn't, Mr. Shakespeare, says the realist. And, with all due deference to Rabbie Burns and Miss Dickinson, my love *isn't* a flower, and hope *doesn't* have feathers. Just the facts, ma'am. Just the facts.

But their hard-headed protests are as metaphorical as the poems they protest. After all, the sound "rose" isn't a flower

THEOPOLITAN READING

either, the sound "feathers" never helped a bird fly, and the sound "breakfast biscuit" never stilled the rumblings of our morning borborygmi.

Every text is poetic because language itself is poetic. Metaphor happens every time we speak. It's the foundation of all language. I see my coffee mug next to my keyboard. I point to it—I'm doing it right now!—and say, "That is a mug." I identify an object on my desk with the sound "mug." But is the ceramic-container-for-coffee *identical* to the sound "mug"? How can an object "be" a sound? By what magic does my treasured coffee-container come to be in a new form within the sentence I'm writing? How can an object "be" the visible markings "m-u-g"?

I can't explain the magic. It's a thing more to be adored than explained. But I know this: If metaphor is an error or a distortion of reality, *everything* we say is hopelessly distorted. Because metaphor lies at the base of all language.

We're the only creatures who do this kind of thing. Chimps signal to each other, Brazil's titi monkeys emit a range of sounds to locate predators, parrots mimic human speech, rats learn to identify letters on the doors of a maze. No other creature, though, uses metaphor. Only *we*, made in the image of God, have the creative power to say, "This (thing) *is* this (sound/visible sign)." We alone can make things in the world exist in a new mode within our speech. We alone are poets, God's *poiema*, mimicking the poetry of the divine Poet.

Paying attention to the poetry of a text isn't something we do "in addition to" getting the meaning. No matter how literal the text, we read it well only if we pay attention to the poetry—the way it's *made*.

Paying attention to the poetry means paying attention to word choices and the overtones and music of each word. Good readers pay attention to how words, like molecules, react and transform in the presence of other words. Good readers

SPIRITUAL READING

have read many texts and hear echoes of one text inside another. Good readers have an ear for how motifs echo and reecho through the whole. Good readers read with all senses on alert, as if their lives depended on getting *everything*.

Let me try an experiment, or a game, to illustrate the magic of words. Let's start with one word:

> robin

What's a good reader to get from that lonely, apparently unpromising word? At least this: A robin is a bird, proverbial harbinger of spring. "Robin" brings to mind the rusty red of the robin's breast feathers. Whatever might be added, we expect springtime, new birth.

Well, good. Let's add another word:

> robin's eggshell

Well, that changes things. The definition of "robin" hasn't changed a bit, but the additional word picks out one aspect of "robin" and focuses our attention *there*. At the same time, it opens a range of new associations: Robin's eggs are sky blue, small, fragile, round, smooth. If we were already thinking spring when we read "robin," we're thinking it even more now since robins lay eggs in springtime. The sound and rhythm of the two words capture our ear. The phrase has a meter and nearly alliterates with different ranges of "s" (from a hard *z* to a softer *sh*).

OK, now we're getting somewhere. Let's add another:

> robin's eggshell fine.

That's a surprise. We've been thinking of the properties of birds and eggshells, but now "robin" and "eggshell" modify the adjective "fine." Some things, perhaps, are "ostrich-egg" fine, which isn't very fine at all, or "turtle-egg" fine, which is leathery.

THEOPOLITAN READING

Whatever this sentence is about, it has a different kind of fineness, similar to the fineness of a tiny bird egg. All we've thought about robins and eggshells still lingers in our minds when we add "fine." Whatever is "fine," it's going to have some of the qualities of the bird and the shell— spring, delicate, perhaps even blue!

Let's end the suspense and quote the whole line:

> The day is robin's eggshell fine.
> ("Lake Ontario Park," Sadiqa de Meijer)

Well, I wasn't expecting *that* at all! Were you? A piece of china, a woman's skin and facial structure, or the sensibility of a delicate, rather nervous Victorian lady might be "robin's eggshell fine." For Sadiqa de Meijer, the phrase describes a *day*. We were right to detect a wisp of meter: This line scans as iambic tetrameter (unstressed-stressed, four times).

Notice what has happened. We started with one word. That one word is part of the English language and so already exists in the context of the whole set of English words. In English, this sound "robin" *is* a certain kind of bird. "Robin" belongs with other animal words, but its sound distinguishes it from other animal words. A robin is not-sparrow, not-hawk, not-alligator, as well as not-granite and not-shotgun

Besides, "robin" has been used millions of times over the centuries and has picked up standard connotations. A good reader hears the reverberations of the word as it occupies its place in the context of the language, the history of English literature, the history of the world.

Then we added other words. We added *more* context. With each additional word, we performed some paradoxical magic. Each new word *limited* the scope of "robin." Adding "eggshell" drew our attention away from the bird, its color or feathers, to its egg. Adding "fine" put the delicacy of the egg-

SPIRITUAL READING

shell in the forefront, rather than its color or shape. We could, after all, say, "His head was robin's eggshell round" or "Her eyes were robin's eggshell blue." Each new word, each additional bit of context, imprisoned the words and directed us down a particular path of reading.

At the same time, the additional context liberates and opens. Each new word opens up fresh connotations and possibilities. We may not have thought of "fragile" as a quality of "robin," but "eggshell" forced that on our attention. Robins aren't blue, but their eggs are.

The sentence offers a new glimpse of reality. I dare say none of you had thought to describe a day as "robin's eggshell fine" before reading that line of poetry. Now that you've read the phrase, you'll experience some days differently. Perhaps you'll be led to the thought that *each* day breaks as a new birth, as springtime, as fragile and as full of promise as a robin's egg. Perhaps you'll ask whether the poem's eggshell is whole or broken and be sobered at the thought that fine newborn days can so easily be shattered into a million little pieces.

Notice we've done all this without leaving the words behind for a moment. The marks on the page, with the attendant sounds and meanings, have been our guide at every step. As we've paid attention to the poetry of the text—to the way the line is constructed and to the materials it's constructed from—these six simple words have dazzled our ears and eyes and trained our senses to engage the world with new delight and insight.

We can also interrogate the line of poetry. What season is it? The line doesn't answer our question, but we infer it's spring. What kind of weather is it? We know it's *fine*, but "eggshell" hints at a brilliant blue sky with few or no clouds. "Fine" doesn't just mean "good weather" but suggests a cool tang in the air. *I* suspect it's morning.

I can't prove that it's spring, or that the sky is blue, or that it's morning. Perhaps the rest of the poem will clarify. With just this one line, a skeptic—perhaps *you*—might ask, "Haven't we read too much into the text?" Wouldn't we be better readers if we said, "No, we can't go beyond what's written. All we know about the day is that it's 'robin's eggshell fine,' whatever that might mean. Anything more is eisegesis"?

At the risk of insulting skeptical readers, the answer is, "No." A response like that comes from a very *bad* reader, a reader who thinks interpretation is no more than paraphrase. It comes from a reader with untrained poetic senses, a childish reader who wants to stay safe, a Peter-Pannish reader who never wants to grow up. To such readers, I can do no more than repeat the hermeneutical exhortation of Jesus, the Model Reader: "Have no fear."

A good reader is like someone with a well-tuned ear for music. A good reader hears the overtones and harmonies, the shifts in meter and instrumentation, that a casual reader misses. A good reader is *not* hearing things—no more than a trained music listener. A good reader notices what's on the page and catches the overtones, connotations, import, and implications of what's written. A good reader is so attentive to the text that he notices the thousands of traces of things that are virtually there. He's so attentive to what's there that he notices what's *not* there.

The Bible as Poetry

If all texts are poems, made-things, the Bible is too. We can be more definite. God wrote Scripture in a mode closer to poetry than to scientific or philosophical prose. The Bible is full of explicit poetry: the songs of the Pentateuch and Judges 5, the book of Psalms and the Song of Songs, long stretches of the prophetic writings. Each is a masterpiece of concentrated excess.

Take this, for instance: "Put me like a seal on your heart, like a seal on your arm," says the Bride in the Song of Songs (8:6).

SPIRITUAL READING

Seals mark things with the name of the owner. To say that the Bride seals the Bridegroom is to say that the Bride stamps her name on him. It's a love metaphor. She wants him to be *hers*.

But this line almost-says more than it says. If we remember the rest of the Song, we know there's *mutual* ownership: I am my beloved's, my beloved is mine (SoS 2:16; 6:3). And if we read the Song as Yahweh's hymn of love to Israel, the scope of the image expands. Surprisingly, the Song emphasizes the *Bride's* ownership of her Husband, that is, *Israel's* ownership of Yahweh. Yahweh is Lord, yet He is so fully devoted to Israel that *she* owns *Him*. The Creator has freely decided He will not be God except as the Bridegroom of Israel.

His heart and arm are sealed. *Heart* because the Bridegroom's heart is captivated by the bride (cf. Song 7:5), *arm* because the arm symbolizes strength—the strength of Yahweh's arm stretched out against Egypt (Exod 6:6; 15:16; Deut 4:34; 5:15; 26:8), the strength of the everlasting arms that defend Israel (Deut 33:17), the strength of the hosts of Yahweh (cf. Dan 11:6). The Bridegroom's strong arm, like His heart, belongs to the Bride.

"Love is as strong as death," Solomon adds, the very "flame of Yah" (SoS 8:6; my translation). Israel's story is a story of a love as strong as *mot*, the god of death. Yahweh's jealousy is as possessive as *sheol* (SoS 8:6), His flame too fiery to be quenched by many waters. Think of the waters that *haven't* quenched Yahweh's love: The waters of creation are no match for the Spirit. Yahweh blows the floodwaters, and dry land appears. With a breath, Yahweh divides the waters at the Red Sea. Yahweh's fire licks the drench from Elijah's altar. Yahweh reaches down to the roots of the earth to draw Jonah from the watery gates of Sheol.

Nothing stands in the way of the flame of Yahweh's love. On the contrary, *everything* is fuel for this fire and only makes the consuming Fire burn brighter, whiter, hotter.

John is the model reader of the Song, for he identifies Jesus as the glorified flame of Yah. Jesus has the keys to "death and Hades" (Rev 1:18). He's Love incarnate, the fire who is not consumed by many waters, the Lover who consumes death in pursuit of His bride. His death and resurrection are the great historical demonstration of Yahweh's passionate devotion to His Bride.

In those few lines, we hear the whole story of Scripture, which is the story of the world. And those few lines, read well, train us to face the waves and floods of life with confidence. Death stares us in the face, but we know His jealousy is harder than *sheol*. An epidemic unsettles *everything*, but this, too, is fuel for Yahweh's love. Scripture trains our senses to sense the world as it actually is.

You might admit that biblical poetry is a concentrated excess. But it's not just the poetry. Even the prose sections of Scripture are highly charged pieces of writing. We pay attention to details and muse on them in the light of the rest of Scripture. We try to hear the overtones and undertones, to pick up subtle shifts in rhythm and the little gestures that point us to other texts. And suddenly, with a flash of insight, we see how the jagged pieces of text fit together, which helps us to discern God's pattern in the fabric of the world.

Another example. What could be more boring and unfruitful than the genealogy of Judah (1 Chr 2)? But we don't have to read far before we recognize the brief stories told in Judah's genealogy as stories of death and resurrection.

Death intrudes early in the genealogy of Judah, Israel's royal tribe. The sons of Judah die because of their wickedness (1 Chr 2:1-4). Notably, this is the first time the Chronicler refers to God. When Yahweh appears, He comes not as Creator but as *killer*, as Judge and Executioner. God is a killer, especially of kings (Chr 10:14; cf. 2 Chr 36:17-18).

Er is so wicked that Yahweh puts him to death (1 Chr 2:3). None of Judah's other sons appear to have children. We know from

SPIRITUAL READING

Genesis that God put Onan to death too (Gen 38), and Shelah's line is (canonically if not historically) aborted. Judah gets a new lease on life through Tamar, his Canaanite daughter-in-law, who bears the twins, Perez and Zerah. The abortive line of Judah is revived through a Gentile.

Then it happens *again*. Zerah's sons are listed then disappear (1 Chr 2:6-8), another abortive line. His descendants end with Achan/Achar, "the troubler of Israel, who violated the ban" (2:7) and was stoned. Zerah, whose name means "rising" and puns on the word for "seed," is *not* fruitful. Another false start; another blind alley for Judah.

Perez, the one who breaks through, has two sons, Hezron and Hamul. The Chronicler's genealogy focuses on the former, whose three sons are Jerameel, Ram, and Chelubai (1 Chr 2:9). Jerahmeel's line through Onam stalls three times over. One line goes from Onam to Seled, who "died without sons" (1 Chr 2:30). Another line from Onam goes through Jada to Jether, who "died without sons" (1 Chr 2:32). Sheshan (1 Chr 2:34) also has no sons, but his line is re-started through his daughter, whom he gives to an Egyptian slave, Jarha (1 Chr 2:34-35). Another death and resurrection for Judah; another renewal linked with the incorporation of Gentiles.

What would Jesus the Model Reader make of this genealogy? As He tells the disciples on the road to Emmaus, everything speaks of Him, including the "boring" genealogy of His tribe. Jesus would tell them, "I am the Risen One, descended from the tribe of resurrection. In Me, Jew and Gentile are knit together, for my tribe is already the beginning of one new, united humanity."

Throughout this reading of 1 Chronicles 2, I've shifted back and forth between "literal" and "figurative" reading. Did Judah's line come close to dying out? Literally, yes. Does that foreshadow something about the tribe of Judah, the line of David, great David's greater Son? Yes again. Am I saying the text is *both* literal

THEOPOLITAN READING

and figurative? That it has *multiple* senses?

Why, yes I am. And I really shouldn't have to defend my viewpoint. Most uses of language are literal and figurative. Am I, to refer back to an earlier sentence, really "defending" anything? Not literally. When I speak of "defending my viewpoint," I operate within the common master metaphor that equates argument with war. To refer back a few pages, was the day literally "fine"? Yes. Was it literally a "robin's eggshell"? Nope. Days aren't eggshells. Does that mean the line is an incoherent train wreck? No. It means the poem mixed figurative and literal, *just as we all do all the time.*

We need to free ourselves from the deranged notion that a text must be either literal or figurative and that we have to read consistently one way or the other. The demand for consistency can only lead to absurdities.

"Babylon" is a great city and a great harlot (Rev 17—18). Which *is* it, John? If it's the city "Babylon," "Harlot" can't be literal. A city might be full of harlots, but the city itself cannot be a harlot. And it's not literally "Babylon" either. By John's day, Babylon wasn't a great power. Both terms are figurative. We can't take either one literally without talking nonsense.

Yet deciding that "Babylon the great harlot" is figurative does *not* mean that there's no literal city. "Babylon" refers, I believe, to a specific city, Jerusalem, that was literally conquered in A.D. 70. Yet, on the other hand, taking "Babylon" as a real city does *not* commit us to taking every detail of John's description literally. John sees Babylon dressed in scarlet and purple, wearing a name on her forehead, drinking blood from a golden cup. We don't need to ask whether cities have foreheads, or whether they can wear clothes, or where you find a city's hand to hold a golden cup.

Yet again, though figures, all of those details have some sort of literal force. The harlot city Babylon kills martyrs, spilling real blood. Her clothing and headgear indicate she's a priestess, and the city is the priestly city Jerusalem. With her idolatries and acts of unfaithfulness, Jerusalem truly is a harlot, albeit not literally so.

John's description is a blessedly bewildering mash of literal and figurative, and as readers we have the priestly-royal privilege of drawing lines and making distinctions. It's a mash of literal figures.

How do we make sense of a text like this? How do we know the difference between literal and figurative? There's no trick, machine, or manual. Start by refusing to polarize the two. Find a mature mentor who is willing to teach you to read. Under his guidance, cultivate a sacramental imagination that can see bread and body, water and Spirit, city and harlot, tree and man, both together at a glance, without division or confusion. And then, armed with a transformed imagination and alerted senses, learn to read.

The Spiritual Reader

To read well, to read in the Spirit, we must cultivate the fruits of the Spirit. Spiritual reading doesn't take place outside us. If there's to be Spiritual reading, there must be Spiritual readers. And Spiritual readers are those who walk in the Spirit in everything. If you want to learn to read well, don't quench the Spirit. Walk in the Spirit. Pray for and practice the fruits of the Spirit. Read in the Spirit.

Love is the first fruit of the Spirit (Gal 5:2). Spiritual readers must read with love. We keep company with neighbors when we keep company with books. Books may be friends or enemies. We're called to love both in the Spirit. When we love someone, we're attentive to his or her needs and desires. When we love a book, we are attentive to the poetry of the text. Reading in the

Spirit, we don't drift from the page every three seconds to check our text messages. Reading in the Spirit, we don't forget the previous chapter when we get to a new one. The Spirit trains our senses to grasp the Bible accurately and fully.

Love is patient (1 Cor 13:4). Reading takes time. Reading in the Spirit, we don't jump to conclusions about what the author is saying. We listen with care to hear what's said and what's unsaid. The best reading, Robert Penn Warren once observed, comes not on the first or fifth or tenth reading but on the hundredth. We read best when we can "remember ahead," knowing the beginning and anticipating the end at every moment. We can do that only if we read, re-read, and re-re-read. We read well only in the patience of the Spirit.

Love is not arrogant (1 Cor 13:4). Reading in the Spirit, we humble ourselves before the author. We let him set the rules. Humility makes our reading playful; we play by the author's rules. When we make ourselves small, the text and the world are enlarged. Mature readers know how to be as children before the text.

The Spirit is the Spirit of creativity. Creativity isn't incompatible with submission to authority. On the contrary, humility is the only possible starting point for creativity. Pride is never creative, except of Pandaemonium.

We cannot produce anything absolutely *ex nihilo*. Though not creative as God is creative, we *are* creative. To be creative, we need to humble ourselves before the materials. A sculptor must submit not only to the characteristics of marble, but to the peculiar shape and features of *this piece* of marble.

Pianists and violinists and ensembles, like composers, are creative artists. Like all artists, performers submit to the material—the *authoritative* composition from the hand of the *author*. True, the notes on the page "limit" the creativity of the performer. If he is going to play *this* Bach fugue, he must play *these* notes, count out *this* rhythm, maintain *this* pace. But the limitation isn't really limitation. It's a necessary step toward freedom. We aren't playing Bach "freely" when we burst through the limits and play whatever notes we please. We're no longer playing Bach at all. As he humbles himself before Bach, the performer can create Bachian music. He limits himself to *these* notes so his music can stretch out to heaven.

Reading is creative in a similar way. We humble ourselves before the text and learn to perform it well. Following a guide, we enter the text and the world that it creates and get to know our way around. We accept its limits. Once we become familiar with the hallways, floor plan, and general layout, we're able to sniff out hidden passageways.

None of this takes place in isolation. The Spirit is *among* us, occupying the space between, not merely *in* each of us. The Spirit gathers. He weds and welds many into one without losing the unique contributions of each. As we noted at the start of the chapter, our senses are trained to read well, and we mature in our ability to read well, in conversation. Spiritual reading is reading in communion.

Literally *communion*. The dialogue that makes us good readers is a liturgical dialogue. We have Bible software and the internet and books galore. Pre-modern readers and teachers had the liturgy. *They* had the advantage.

Medieval monks spent their days in the scriptorium, copying and studying texts. They chanted the entire Psalter each week and listened to large chunks of the Bible during their hours of prayer. The Bible entered their souls through their eyes, but God's Word chimed in their ears, and they tasted it in their mouths.

Sadly, it's impossible to replicate that kind of experience in many Protestant churches. Many churches with "Bible" in their name have little Bible in worship. Their hymns contain isolated snatches of Scripture. The pastor reads a few verses for his sermon text, but otherwise the Bible is a closed book, unread and unheard. By a weird irony, many traditionally liturgical churches are more immersed in Scripture than Bible-believing Evangelical ones. You'll hear more Bible at a Catholic Mass or an Orthodox Divine Service than you will at many Bible churches.

The Bible is solid food, but you need to mature in the Spirit to digest it. Within the liturgy, Scripture brings us to maturity. To become a Spiritual reader, you need to take up and read. You need to take note and *hear*.

2 WORLD

To see Your power and Your glory.
Psalm 63:2

God is the Hero of Scripture, the main character and actor. He creates. He sends the flood. He calls Abraham. He rescues Israel from Egypt and clears Canaanites out of Israel's land. He crowns David and gives splendor to Solomon. He drives Israel into exile and brings them up again. In the last days, He comes in person to establish Himself as King and Savior of Israel and the nations, revealing Himself as Father, Son, and Spirit.

Yet the God of the Bible is the Creator and Ruler of the *world*. The Bible is about God-with-the-world, rarely about God-in-isolation. We learn many, many things about God, but we learn them through His interaction with creation. We know God in His effects.

The Bible's worldliness is a surprise to people who don't know much about the Bible—sadly, even to many Christians. They expect a book about spiritual things, eternity, and heaven. They expect a *religious* book in the attenuated modern sense that defines "religion" as private, individual piety. Some expect a book

THEOPOLITAN READING

about God-in-Himself.

What they find instead is a book about human beings, about earth and time, about bodies—a *this*-worldly book. The Bible is about aging parents longing desperately for their first children, about sibling rivalry, about political clashes between God and kings, about war and conquest, about exile and return. People come expecting a book about heaven and find the Bible is of the earth, earthy.

Scripture's laws don't look spiritual. God tells Israel how to treat slaves and punish thieves and care for the landless poor (Exod 21—23). He gives detailed instructions to help priests distinguish varieties of skin disease (Lev 13—14) and spends an embarrassing amount of time on genital emissions (Lev 15). His law prescribes who may have sex with whom and the penalties for violation (Lev 18, 20). There are rules for worship (Lev 1—7), but they don't look very spiritual either, what with all the slaughter, dismemberment, entrails, blood, fire, vapor, and smoke.

The Bible's principal characters aren't monks or mystics or hermits or scholars but men of the world—shrewd sheiks, bold shepherds, deliverers, chest-thumping judges, priests, kings, and prophets. The women of the Bible are pious, but their piety is practical and political: They pray for children and for social revolution (1 Sam 2:1-11; Luke 1:46-56), lie to protect the innocent, and sometimes reach for a hammer and spike to split an enemy's skull. Israel's prophets don't do much in the way of calculating the timing of the rapture. They're intensely engaged in the politics of their day. They instruct and rebuke kings and deliver God's interpretation of current events.

For many, the New Testament seems to be a different, more agreeable sort of book. Jesus goes to isolated places for long nights of prayer. He tells His disciples to love one another, condemns the rich and tells them to give their goods to the poor, and encourages all to trust His Father's care. He teaches His disciples how to pray and seems to avoid the messy politics of first-century Judea.

That's more like it. That's what religion *really* is.

But it's an optical illusion. The Bible is mostly Old Testament, and we can't disengage the two Testaments without distorting both. Besides, the Gospels are mostly taken up with Jesus' *public* ministry of preaching, exorcism, healing, and teaching. His main message is a political one: "The kingdom of God is at hand." God is taking charge of the world, and He's doing it through Jesus; therefore, everyone, including rulers, had better get ready for a change of regime. Jesus provokes titanic clashes with the Jewish establishment, and the battle in the temple so enrages the leaders that they plot (successfully) to kill Him.

At some point, someone decided John's Gospel was the most "spiritual" of the four. Whoever made that decision hadn't read the Gospel very carefully. In chapter after chapter, Jesus performs a sign and then gets into a verbal war with Jewish leaders who object to what He's done (John 4—11). John is the most litigious, the most contentious of the four Gospels.

This *is* spirituality. Jesus is the One born of the Spirit (John 3:1-8). But it's not the kind of soft spirituality we expect if we're used to looking at Sunday school picture books or watching Jesus movies.

The earthly focus of the Bible continues right to the end. Revelation tells us more about heaven than the rest of the Bible combined (cf. chs. 4—5, 8, 15). But at the climax of Revelation, our attention is again drawn toward earth. Instead of ending with a vision of heaven, Revelation ends with visions of a heavenly city *descending to earth* (Rev 21—22).

Long ago, Christians developed the mental tick of ignoring the obvious, of switching registers, of "raising" our minds from the earthiness of Scripture to heavenly and spiritual things. We've developed the habit of translating stories about barrenness and sibling rivalry and politics and war into stories about the

THEOPOLITAN READING

lonely journey of the soul. We've insisted on turning the Bible into the kind of religious book we expect or want it to be.

But the surface story of the Bible *is* the story of the Bible. The Bible isn't a book about heaven or eternity or spiritual things. It's a story of heaven-and-earth, eternity-and-time, of the Spirit's formation and re-formation of matter. The Bible's content is mostly about the second term in each of those pairs. Most of the Bible's sentences and stories, most of its poems and prophecies, are about earth, time, and men and women with real bodies and souls.

The Bible doesn't turn us away from history but gives us a *reading* of history, God's own telling of the story of Himself-with-His-world. The Bible isn't about how we can go to heaven when we die. It's not about how we can escape the prison of this world. It's about the formation, deformation, restoration, and glorification of God's creation. It's the good news that heaven has invaded and conquered earth. We don't read and study Scripture so we can escape the world. Spiritual readers study to train our senses to understand the world and history more deeply.

Even when Paul exhorts us to raise our minds to heavenly things (Col 3:1-6), it's not for the reason we might expect. We focus on heaven because that's where *Jesus* reigns—Jesus, the Word made *flesh*, Jesus the God-*man*, Jesus with His glorified *body*. As soon as Paul directs our hearts to heaven, he gives instructions about how to live out our personal relationships on earth (Col 3:8-17). We don't leave earth behind when we raise our minds to heaven. We look ahead to earth's future. Heaven is where the future happens first. We turn to heaven not to escape earth but to contemplate earth's destiny. And we contemplate that destiny so we can pray and labor until His will is done on earth as in heaven.

World as Word

When the Bible turns our attention to the world, it's *not* turning us away from God. His eternal power and divine nature are clearly seen in what He made (Rom 1:18-32). Creation comes from the God of eternal glory and is a temporal, created radiance of that glory. That's what the world *is*.

Everything in creation manifests God. He is light (1 John 1:5) and speaks light (Gen 1:4-6). He is brighter than the sun (Psa 84:11), which every day blazes like the divine Bridegroom across the sky (Psa 19:5). Every fire and every cloud reveal the God who appears to Israel in cloud and fire (Exod 13:21). His storm rests on Sinai and shoots lightning bolts as arrows (Psa 18:14). He is fiercer and stronger than a lion, gentler than a lamb. His Spirit flutters like an eagle (Deut 32:11) and a dove (Matt 3:16). His voice is like the sound of many waters, the roaring of the sea (Ezek 1:24).

Trees link earth and heaven, like the Son of Man who straddles sea and land (Rev 10:1-2). Dew evaporates in an hour, but while it lasts it sparkles like a precious gem, refracting divine glory. Clouds are airy nothings, yet God paints sunsets with them, so they gleam with His grandeur. Birds flit and sing like the angels of heaven, and the Creator shows His kindness by providing for the worms and roaches that slither and scuttle at our feet.

At the end, the world becomes transparent to the glory of God when in the new Jerusalem, God Himself replaces the sun and moon as light source (Rev 21:23). In the end, the world, matured into a heavenly city, will shine even more fully with the brilliance of divine glory. The Bible is the story of the world's advance from glory to glory.

Made in the image of God, men and women especially manifest the glory of God. He who made the eye sees; He who made the ear hears; He who made the mouth speaks (Psa 94:8-11).

His arms and hands are strong to save (Exod 7:4-5). His feet rest on the circle of heaven (Isa 40:22).

Human artifacts and actions reveal God. He is a shield (Psa 84:11) and a fortress (Psa 18:10). His voice shakes the earth like a marching army (Ezek 1:24). He's like a man overcome with wine, who wakes suddenly and starts breaking things (Psa 78:65-68). Jeremiah complains that Yahweh is a deceptive spring, which promises refreshment but gives none (Jer 15:18).

Every time you see a human being, every time you see *anything*, you're encountering a revelation of God. God speaks. God speaks the world into being. Coming from His speech, the world echoes and answers the Creator. God speaks to the creature through the creature. Our speech is always a translation of God's prior speech. If you don't see this, you're seeing an illusion and not the world as it is. If you don't see the glory of God when you peer outside your eyeballs, you're insane. You need new eyes, ears, hands, and a new nose and tongue. You need your senses healed, trained, and tuned to reality.

Sometimes theologians say the Bible's language is "accommodated." God "lisps" to us as we do to infants because we can't handle anything more.

That's not entirely false. God *is* gracious in His speech. He speaks in a way we can understand. But for readers like the medieval Jewish philosopher Maimonides or the early modern critic Benedict Spinoza, accommodation means something different. For them, Scripture's language is inadequate or second-best. Many modern readers of Scripture say that talking about God as "shield" and "sun" is childish. It's *not*. It's the way God has chosen to speak about Himself. It's a fitting way for God to describe Himself because God originally created sun, sea, shields and everything else to shout and sing of Him. Even before He speaks of Himself as "sun," the sun already speaks of Him. The Bible only reminds us of what is already true.

Maimonides and Spinoza and their Christian heirs also complain about the Bible's use of "anthropomorphisms," descriptions of God in human terms. Some think these are childish too and say we need to outgrow them. Anthropomorphisms aren't childish. God describes Himself in human terms because humans are made in His image. God doesn't have eyes as we have eyes, but He sees. He doesn't have ears like ours, but He hears. Better, we should say, "He's the original, and we are the copies." He has the *original* ears, eyes, mouth, hands, arms, feet. Our bodily organs are glorious copies of God's more glorious powers.

We can't grasp Scripture without knowing something about the world. We can't understand what it means for God to be "sun" without knowing something about the sun. We won't quake at the Lord's thunderous voice (Psa 29) unless we've heard thunder. Our life experience trains our senses and so prepares us for the solid food of Scripture. It works the other way too. We can't grasp the world rightly without Scripture. Only the mature with trained senses can stand solid food, but Scripture trains our senses so we hear, see, touch, smell, and taste the world as it actually is. Spiritual reading of Scripture makes us good readers of the world.

As we saw in chapter 1, all language is inherently metaphorical. Every time we speak, we speak of the world "as" something else. We speak of flying things with the sound "bird" and fluffy-tailed climbing things with the sound "squirrel." The Bible teaches us how to speak rightly of the world. It teaches us to see everything "as" a finite form of God's infinite glory. Because everything *is* just that.

Three-Story House

The Bible's focus on earth is plain from the first chapters. As soon as we're introduced to God, we're introduced to His world: "In the beginning, God created the heavens and the earth"

(Gen 1:1). The next sentence turns our attention to earth: "Now the *earth* was formless and void" (Gen 1:2). That's where our attention stays for the rest of Genesis 1 and into Genesis 2 and 3 and on through most of the Bible.

The whole Bible grows from the seeds planted in Genesis 1—3. The patterns, persons, and events of the early chapters of the Bible set the trajectory for the whole story. Every man is a variation on Adam, every woman a daughter of Eve, every environment an Eden or a ruined Eden, a wilderness. To read the Bible well, we have to have the first chapters firmly in our minds. That's the aim of the remainder of this book.

At the beginning, creation is nothing but dark *tohu wabohu*, "formless-and-void-ness" (Gen 1:2). Over the course of the creation week, God transforms all of those conditions. First, He calls light into existence to dispel the darkness; then He forms the formless; finally, He fills the empty form. He switches on the lights, builds the house, and then moves in the furniture.

He spends roughly the first half of the creation forming. God calls out into the undifferentiated darkness, "Let there be light," and there is light. He separates light and darkness so that they dance out nights and days (Gen 1:3-5). God gives creation a temporal form—its rhythm and harmonies.

Then He turns to forming space, which is primarily a hydraulic operation. He hauls water from earth up to heaven and then separates the waters above from the waters below with a firmament (Gen 1:6-8). At the beginning of Day 3, He divides the waters that remain on earth so that dry land appears (Gen 1:9-10). Creation is an art of boundary-making.

By the middle of the third day, God has created a three-story cosmic house. There's a firmament above, called "heaven." Earth is beneath the firmament, and below the earth are the waters of the sea.

Throughout Scripture, the phrase "heaven, earth, and waters

under the earth" means "everything in the visible creation." The Second Word prohibits Israel from making and bowing to anything "in heaven above, or on the earth beneath, or in the waters under the earth" (Exod 20:4). Yahweh is the One who "builds His upper chambers in the heavens, and has founded His vaulted dome over the earth" and "who calls for the waters of the sea" (Amos 9:6). He brings universal judgment when He shakes "the heavens and the earth, the sea also and the dry land" (Hag 2:6) or when He empties the earth of beasts, the sky of birds, and the sea of fish (Zeph 1:2-3).

When seven angels trumpet their trumpets, the Lamb burns the earth with fiery hail (Rev 8:8) then tosses a mountain into the sea that turns the ocean to blood (Rev 8:10). A star falls into the springs of water, poisoning the rivers (Rev 8:10), and when the fourth angel sounds, the lights of the firmament blink out (Rev 8:12). When all is said and done, each story of the cosmos has been demolished.

When all is going well, these zones of creation remain distinct and bounded. Heavenly waters stay in heaven, and the sea politely observes the boundary of the shore. When God removes the boundaries, the world returns to an undifferentiated primordial soup. Seeing the violence of the world, He removes the firmament barrier and lets deadly rain loose on the world in the flood. After forty days and nights of rain, with additional water bubbling up from beneath the sea, the world is back to its original state—a watery emptiness (Gen 7–9).

Sometimes the firmament cracks and crashes to the earth as giant hailstones (Exod 9:18-34; Isa 28:2, 17; Rev 8:7; 11:19; 16:21). Yahweh rips the veil of the sky as He comes to see, discern, and pass judgment, and to help and rescue His faithful ones (Isa 64:1). Jeremiah cuts to the chase. Heaven goes dark, and the earth quakes as the world slips back into its original formless-and-void-ness, the *tohu wabohu* that existed before God's voice pierced the darkness (Jer 4:23-26).

Every time you read about something happening to "heaven, earth, and sea" in Scripture, you're reading about a worldwide something. Every time you see the boundaries between heaven, earth, and sea dissolve, you're watching creation-in-reverse. God de-forms what He once formed.

Conversely, when God puts boundaries back in place, He's re-forming and re-creating. When flood waters top the mountains, Yahweh remembers Noah and sends a "wind" to uncover the earth (Gen 8:1). The Hebrew word for "wind" is *ruach*, the same as the word for "Spirit." Genesis 8:1 is a replay of Genesis 1:2, with the Spirit-wind over the deep re-forming the world. When Israel is trapped at the Red Sea, Yahweh divides the waters to make a path of dry land (Exod 14:21-22), replicating the work of the third day of creation. He shakes down the old world of Egypt so He can form the new creation of Israel (cf. Psa 77:16-20).

The Bible teaches us to see the cosmos as a three-story *house*. Scripture attributes architectural features to the cosmos. Heaven has foundations (2 Sam 22:8), and so does earth (Psa 82:5; 104:5), laid by the Architect and Builder of creation (Isa 51:13). The earth is set on pillars (1 Sam 2:8; Job 9:6; Psa 75:3). The firmament is a starry dome over our heads (Amos 9:6).

Nations are small-scale creations, constructed by creative boundary-making. God sits as King on the circle of the heavens, and the king shines in the firmament of the people. The people are earth, and their enemies are the seas that threaten to overwhelm them. Israel especially is the people of land, and the Gentile nations are often pictured as a surging, turgid ocean. Yahweh sometimes allows the sea to flood the land (Isa 8:6-8), but then He speaks again, and Israel emerges as dry land from the midst of the sea. The micro-creation of Israel is de-formed, then re-formed.

God's various sanctuaries replicate the three-story structure of creation. With its three decks, Noah's ark is a small cosmos (Gen 6:16). The tabernacle and temple are divided into three zones—the court, the Holy Place (or "nave"), and the Most Holy Place (or, in King James English, the "oracle"). Each is a small cosmos, training our eyes to see the world as a cosmic temple.

These uses of the cosmic symbolism of heaven, earth, and sea clarify what's happening in various passages of Scripture. When Jeremiah says the world is slipping back into an empty void, he's not necessarily talking about the end of the physical universe. We have to look at the context. When we do, it's clear he's warning that Yahweh will demolish *Judah's* world, not planet Earth (Jer 4:22, 27-31).

Yahweh threatens to strip sky, land, and sea, but Zephaniah makes it clear He's stretching out His hand against Judah and Jerusalem (Zeph 1:1-6). The trumpets of the trumpet angels dismantle earth, sea, rivers, and land, but Revelation is about things that happened soon after John sees the visions (Rev 1:1-2). John isn't seeing visions of the end of the universe. He's seeing visions of the end of the old world.

To read well, we need to read bifocally, or trifocally, remembering that the world is a house, is a temple, is a political order. And then, having read Scripture, we need to see the world bifocally, seeing it "as" a stable or collapsing house, a glorious or a ruined temple. In this way, Scripture trains our senses to have contact with the world as it truly is.

Furniture of Creation

After the Lord forms the world into heaven, earth, and sea, He begins to fill it. In the middle of Day 3, He commands the earth to sprout vegetation. Day 4 fills the firmament with sun, moon, and stars. On Day 5, He creates swimming things in the sea and flying things that fly across the firmament and nest on the land.

THEOPOLITAN READING

On day 6, God calls land animals from the earth and creates man, male and female, in His image and likeness.

Genesis 1 isn't simply telling us that God created all these things. It shows us how these things interconnect.

On Day 1, God creates light, and for the first three days, light comes and goes without any light-giving bodies in the firmament. Presumably, the light comes from God Himself. (Where *else* would it come from?) On Day 4, God delegates this light-giving task to the sun, moon and stars. He gives them authority to "rule" the day and night (Gen 1:16), as He will later delegate authority to man to "rule" birds, fish, and animals (Gen 1:26). Heavenly lights rule from the sky as human beings rule on earth.

On Day 3, God calls up fruitful plants (Gen 1:11-12), and on Day 6, He commands man to "be fruitful" (Gen 1:28). We're to imitate the fecundity of the original fruitful things. On Day 5, God "creates" (Gen 1:21; Heb. *bara'*) great sea monsters, as He "creates" heaven and earth (Gen 1:1) and man (Gen 1:27; *bara'* used three times). By virtue of special "creation," sea monsters and man are linked. Land animals come from the same earth as man, on the same day, and so are related to and symbolic of man.

Within the creation account itself, we're given hints of the associations of plants and man, of heavenly lights and man, of fish and man, of birds and man. The creation account gives the main coordinates for a way of looking at everything in creation as meaningful for us. The rest of Scripture fills this out, describing in more detail how the furniture of creation represents us, even as it manifests the glory of God. It all coheres in Jesus, who is both the glorious Creator and the imaging creature.

Biblical Botany

Plants come from the earth bearing fruit in response to God's word (Gen 1:11-12) as man comes from earth and is commanded to be fruitful (Gen 1:28). Plants are the first fruitful things God calls from the earth. Types of men and women are symbolized by species of plants. Righteous men and women are like strong trees, planted by nourishing streams of water, bearing fruit and living long in the green of youth (Psa 1:3). The wicked aren't trees but chaff, the detritus of plants blown away by the wind (Psa 1:4), or grass, which withers and dies as soon as it's grown (Psa 92:7). Indeed, *all* flesh is grass (Psa 40:7-8).

Some people are thorn bushes (Gen 3:18), like Abimelech, who covets kingship only because, unlike the olive tree and the grapevine, he produces no delightful or useful fruit (Judg 9:7-15). Trees are different. Trees stand on the ground and stretch upright to heaven, just like human beings. Trees have "trunks" and "arms" and are topped with a bushy head of glory, just like human beings. No wonder kings are trees (e.g., Dan 4) because in their majesty they link heaven and earth. Trees are ladders to heaven. And thus, Jesus is the tree of life.

Great trees can come crashing down, reduced to stumps (Dan 4). The Lord sends woodsmen with axes to chop down the trees (Isa 10:1-19) and to turn temples to kindling (Psa 74:1-11). David's own house is chopped down to the roots, down to Jesse, as if David never existed (Isa 11:1), until Yahweh brings new growth, a new tree, from the old (Isa 11:1-5). Israel is an olive tree, its roots in the fathers and into which wild Gentiles are grafted (Rom 11:11-24). As olive tree, Israel provides the oil that will illumine the nations, turning them into bright lamps burning with the Spirit.

The entirety of biblical history takes place among trees—Eden's tree of life and the tree of knowledge, the site of Adam's sin (Gen 2:16-17; 3:1-7); the tree of the cross (Gal 3:13) that springs up with new life in the resurrection so we can once again eat from the tree of life in a new Jerusalem (Rev 22:1-5).

This isn't poetic ornamentation on the biblical story.

THEOPOLITAN READING

The *substance* of the biblical story runs through trees and plants. The Bible isn't showing us a "spiritual dimension" to the real world. It gives us the key to unlock the significance of the real world of plants. The trees of Scripture are real trees but bursting with meaning. Genesis 1 not only teaches us how to read the Word; it teaches us how to read the *world*.

Heavenly Lights

Sun, moon, and stars are set in the firmament on Day 4 to rule day and night, to mark seasons and times, and to serve as signs. Human rulers are pictured as heavenly lights. Yahweh promises Abraham his children will be like the stars of heaven (Gen 15:5; 22:17; 26:4). This doesn't just mean he will have *many* descendants. It prophesies the status and quality of his descendants. Abraham will be the father of kings (Gen 17:6).

Sun, moon, and twelve constellations represent Jacob, Rachel, and the sons of Jacob (Gen 37:9-11). David's throne is like the sun before Yahweh (Psa 89:36). When we lift our eyes to heaven, we, like Abraham, see the story of our people.

When Yahweh returns after exile, Zion will no longer need the sun or moon. Yahweh will be their permanent light. Because Yahweh is Zion's Husband, because Zion reflects the light of God, the light that shines in Zion is *"your* light," turning Zion into the light of the world (Isa 60:19-20).

Because heavenly lights symbolize rulers, the blotting out or fall of lights represents the fall of kings and rulers and the collapse of a political order. "The stars of heaven and their constellations will not flash forth their light. The sun will be dark when it rises and the moon will not shed its light," Isaiah says (Isa 13:10). The collapse of outer space? No. The fall of Babylon (Isa 13:1).

"Immediately after the tribulation of those days the sun will be darkened, and the moon will not give its light, and the stars will fall from the sky, and the powers of the heavens will be shaken," Jesus says, quoting Isaiah (Matt 24:29). The end of the world? Nope. The fall of the temple and Jerusalem (Matt 24:1-3).

When the fourth angel trumpets, John sees "a third of the sun and a third of the moon and a third of the stars" are struck (Rev 8:12). End of the world? Not at all. A catastrophe that took place soon after John saw the visions.

This isn't "mere metaphor." These are literal figures. Events are taking place—real catastrophes. And these catastrophes *do* mark the end of a world—the end of a temple order, or the end of a dynasty, or the end of an empire. When we read the Bible bifocally, through the double lenses of Genesis 1, we begin to see political events rightly: as cosmic, earth-shaking events.

All things in heaven hold together in Jesus. He is the Bridegroom-Sun, the bright morning star. He ascends to heavenly places to rule and to govern times and seasons. Creation reveals the glory of God, and Jesus *is* that glory.

Ornitheology and Ichtheology

Birds were created on Day 5, along with swarmers of the sea. Insofar as they occupy the upper region of earth, birds are linked with heavenly lights and with angels, who are also winged. Though birds fly across the firmament, they are also earth-dwellers. They are, in fact, the *first* earth dwellers (Gen 1:22). Birds mediate between earth and heaven.

Birds manifest the Spirit (Gen 1:2). The Spirit "hovers" over the waters, undulating like a winged bird. The only other use of the verb is in Deuteronomy 32, where it describes the movement of a nesting eagle (Deut 32:11). The Spirit is "over the face of the deep"; on Day 3, Elohim makes plants "on the face of the earth"; birds fly "on the face of the firmament."

Birds' wings image winged Yahweh ("I carried you on eagles' wings," Exod 19:4).

A dove brings an olive branch to Noah, a sign that new creation is emerging from the waters. The dove is a messenger/mediator that flies through the air to link Noah to the renewed earth. The scene again links birds with the Spirit: The dove hovers over the waters as the Spirit did (Gen 8:8-12). It's no accident that the Spirit appears as a dove at Jesus' baptism. The bird/Spirit analogy is baked into creation and knit into history.

Abram cuts covenant with animals and birds (Gen 15), confirming the promise of land and an abundant seed. The seed will be like stars and sand, which parallel the land animals and birds of the covenant ceremony. Sand : stars :: cattle : birds :: people : kings.

All Israelites are birds with tassels on the "wings" of their robes (Num 15:37-41). They are Yahweh's flock, also his bevy of doves and his kit of pigeons, sometimes his murder of crows. Israel is winged because it's a heavenly people, dwelling on earth but with a unique connection to heaven. Priests especially are linked with mediating birds as they move between earth and the "heaven" of the sanctuary.

Birds and fish form a Day 5 pair. Birds fly across the face of the firmament. Fish occupy the lowest space of earth, the sea. Because the sea represents the nations, fish represent Gentiles. Big fish are big Gentiles, like the Assyrian empire (Jon 3) or Nebuchadnezzar of Babylon (Jer 51:34) or Pharaoh (Psa 74:13-14; Ezek 29:3). Jesus is the Fisher King. Unlike most Old Testament heroes, He eats *fish* and sends out His "fishers of men" on sea adventures (like Paul's) to reel in the Gentiles.

Once we focus our eyes on birds and fish, we can fill out a political scheme based on creation. Fish occupy the lowest parts of the earth, beasts are on the land, and birds mediate between land and sky. That is, fish are Gentiles, land animals are Israel, birds are angelic priests.

This symbolism is behind the use of birds in the Levitical system. Herd animals represent leaders, and flock animals represent members of the people. Poor people (Lev 5:7, 11; 12:8) and lepers (Lev 14:1-9) offer birds. Offerings of birds bring the marginal from the margins into the presence of God. This fits with the priest-bird symbolism. If lepers are marginal in being outside, priests occupy the other margin, standing as far inside as it's possible to be. Both margins portray the place of Israel in the world: a "marginal" nation chosen to bring the nations to the Creator.

Beasts and Cattle

Land animals are at the center of human vocation. While the Lord gave man dominion over fish and birds, land animals are nearer to and more intertwined with human life. Most birds fly free, and most fish are outside human control. Many land animals have been domesticated.

God *created* some animals domesticated, the animals Scripture describes as "cattle" (*behemah*)—flock animals like sheep and goats, herd animals like bovines, domesticated work animals like donkeys and camels. "Beasts" are wild animals, which begin outside human rule but are brought under human control over time. In the first act of dominion, Adam previews the end by naming both "cattle" and "beasts" (Gen 2:20).

Adam's sin is an inversion of his proper relation to beasts and "creeping things." Instead of taking control and protecting Eve from the serpent, he allows it to trick her into eating the fruit. Because of their subjection to a beast, Adam and Eve become beasts, clothed in animal skins as they leave the garden (Gen 3:21).

That animal clothing replaces the plant clothing, the fig leaf aprons, that Adam and Eve make for themselves. Animal skins are a blessing, covering the shame of human nakedness.

Covering-by-animal is one of the keys to the Mosaic sacrificial system, where an animal is slaughtered and turned to smoke on the altar in order to "cover" or "atone for" sin. The whole sacrificial system is rooted in the created analogy between man and beast.

Different species of animals represent different kinds of people. Kings are supposed to be lions, ferocious protectors of their pride and dangerous to their enemies (Gen 49:9; Rev 5:5). Samson and David demonstrate their prowess by killing lions (Judg 14:5-9; 1 Sam 17:34-37). If they can kill lions, they can successfully battle Philistines. As the lion king, David gathers leonine warriors who share his strength and skill in combat (1 Chr 12:8).

Other men are violent scavengers, jackals who prey on the weak or sneak into abandoned cities to pick through the garbage (Isa 13:22; 34:13). Imagery like this could well be literal. During the coronavirus outbreak of 2020, wild boars and coyotes wandered through empty cities. When human society breaks down, wild animals move in. But the imagery is also symbolic. When the king is not a lion, predatory men roam freely, preying on their defenseless sheep.

Other people are serpents, who kill with the poison under their tongues (Psa 58:4; 140:3). The righteous who trust in the Lord mimic the Seed of the woman and crush the heads of the serpentine wicked (Gen 3:15; Psa 91:13). Groups of animals represent groups of people, which is why Abraham, Isaac, Jacob, Moses, and David start as shepherds and herdsmen before leading the "flock of God" (cf. Ezek 34:15, 17; Zech 9:16; 1 Pet 5:2). Other groups are like packs of dogs, roaming the streets and baring their teeth against the righteous (Psa 22:16; 59:6, 14).

A social taxonomy is built into the sacrificial system. Israel offers only domesticated animals—animals from the flock or herd. Animals for the sin offering are specified according to the offerer's status in Israel (Lev 4). A priest has to offer a bull

(Lev 4:3), a leader a male goat (4:23), and a common person a female goat (Lev 4:28). Male animals represent leaders, and female animals represent the people of Israel, the bride of Yahweh.

The rules of clean and unclean animals also lay out a social taxonomy. Clean domesticated animals may be sacrificed and represent Israel as a priestly people. Many clean animals, though, cannot be offered on the altar, including "the deer, the gazelle, the roebuck, the wild goat, the ibex, the antelope and the mountain sheep" (Deut 14:5). These represent Gentiles who worship Yahweh without becoming part of the priestly people. Israel may become "one flesh" with these animals by eating them just as they may have close communion with God-fearing Gentiles.

On the other hand, some domesticated animals (donkeys, camels, pigs) and many wild animals (all predators, rodents) are unclean. Israelites are neither to eat them nor to touch their corpses.

The curse on the serpent is in the background: "On your belly shall you go, and dust you shall eat all the days of your life" (Gen 3:14). Man is made of dust and is cursed to return to dust (Gen 3:19). If the serpent is a dust-eater, he's a man-eater, an agent of the curse who drags Adam's children down to the dust of death. Land animals that walk in the cursed dust are serpentine, and Israel is forbidden to eat them. Animals with hooves to protect them from the curse-bearing dust are clean.

When David describes his enemies as "strong bulls," "lions," and "dogs," his metaphor isn't arbitrary (Psa 22:11-21). "Bulls" are priests. "Lions" are kings and other civil rulers. "Dogs" are scavenging mobs. David is under assault from "church," state, and the mob. The Psalm isn't a generic prophecy of the suffering of Jesus but a precise animal parable, for Jesus is the object of assault from precisely these three beasts.

Sometimes beasts become monstrous. John sees two beasts,

one from the sea and one from the land (Rev 13:1-10). The sea beast is a Gentile power, picturing Rome (cf. Dan 7:1-8), while the land beast is a Jewish figure, representing Jews who have sold their souls to Roman power. Together, empire and false church kill and devour the saints, just as Romans and Jews allied to destroy Jesus.

Seven Days

Creation is spatially structured as a three-story house—a residence for plants, heavenly lights, birds, fish, and animals. But creation isn't a static, motionless thing. Not for a nano-moment. Even its making takes time. God could have spoken the whole ordered universe into being with a word, but He chose not to. He instead built the world over the course of six days, capping His work with a day of rest and glory. Creation is made in movement, and it continues moving. It's not only an architectural wonder. It's a musical wonder, a billion-voiced symphony of harmonious moments.

Genesis 1 lays out the basic melody of history, a seven-note sequence that is repeated over and over in Scripture. It's the rhythm of creation because it's the rhythm of the Spirit, who is Himself a "seven" (Rev 1:4; 3:1; 4:5; 5:6). The Spirit who equips the Servant of Yahweh with seven graces (Isa 11:1-5) hovers over the waters of the deep. He initiates the rhythm of evenings and mornings, weeks, months, and years. Under the baton of the Spirit, time drums a seven-beat dance.

This is the root of "typology." Typology isn't simply a way of reading. It's not simply the trick of spotting Jesus hidden like Waldo in unlikely texts. Typology is a theology of history.

God has habits. Nothing He does is ever *exactly* the same as before. No day of creation is identical to any other day. But there's a recurring rhythm as God takes, speaks, tears apart, rearranges, and pronounces good. And as the years roll by, He repeats the same actions. He takes hold of a corrupted world, undoes it in the flood, then remakes it. When Israel turns to idols in the time of Judges, Yahweh tears apart His sanctuary, sending part to Gibeah and the other part (eventually) to Jerusalem. When the temple is defiled, He dismantles it and sends it to Babylon so that it can later be returned to the land and rebuilt. Worlds end in a formless void, but then the Spirit breathes new life.

Types of Jesus aren't isolated pictures of a coming Messiah. We spot "types" of Jesus and the church in the Bible because the Bible and the history it records run in cycles. We spot types of Jesus because God keeps forming new Adams from the dust of the ground, building new Eves, setting them in new Edens, until He sends the Last Adam. We spot Jesus again and again because the Spirit keeps beating out his seven-day tempo.

Many Bible teachers say the number 7 is the number of "fullness." That may be true but doesn't tell us much. And it's the wrong way to read the poetry of Scripture. It's a move from a concrete number (7) to an abstract quality ("fullness").

Bible teachers make this move a lot. The desert represents "testing." Lions represent "strength" or "destructive power." White symbolizes "purity." In each case, we move from something we can sense—a place we can survey, a color we can see, a number we can count, an animal that could rip us to shreds—to some quality that we can only think about.

The Bible doesn't work like that. It doesn't move from body to mind, or from matter to Spirit, or from concrete to abstract. Instead, the Bible connects one body with another—one thing, event, or person to another. We move from one concrete reality to another to another, seeing each in the light of the others. Scripture doesn't move us away from our senses but trains them.

The desert has specific qualities, but when a desert is mentioned in Scripture it evokes a set of specific episodes—Israel's journey from Egypt to the land, Elijah's retreat, John the

Baptist, and Jesus' temptations. "White" doesn't represent some abstract quality but draws together the color of manna, the white skin of the leper, the white of a laundered garment, the white robes of the heavenly choir. "Lion" doesn't simply conjure a few leonine qualities but reverberates with prophecies and events throughout the Bible.

When Scripture employs sevenfold patterns, it isn't evoking thoughts of "fullness" or "completeness." It's evoking thoughts of "God's acts in creating the world." Sevenfold patterns are re- or de-creation patterns. For instance,

- Yahweh's instructions for making the tabernacle (Exod 25–31) are laid out in seven speeches, each marked by the words "God spoke to Moses, saying." God created the world through seven days of speech. He creates a new world, the tabernacle, by speaking seven times to Moses who, in obedience to the Word of Yahweh, makes a new world.
- Each action of the priestly ordination ends with the phrase "as Yahweh commanded Moses" (Lev 8:4, 9, 13, 17, 21, 29, 36). The clause appears seven times, hinting that Aaron and his sons are being made "new men" through the ordination rite.
- Seven feasts are listed in the calendar of Leviticus 23. Each year cycles through a creation-week of appointed times.
- The long central vision of Revelation (Rev 4–16) is organized around a series of seven events: Seven seals open to seven trumpets, which climax in the outpouring of seven bowls. In each sequence, the world is undone, un-created, and returned to the formless void.
- Solomon's wisdom is manifested in a sevenfold manner: his house, his food, the seating arrangements, the "standing" of his table servants, the attire of his table servants, his cupbearers, and the "ascent" into the house of Yahweh (1 Kgs 10:4-5).
- No army in Israel's history is as well-equipped as Uzziah's, each warrior being issued a sevenfold panoply of offensive and defensive arms (2 Chr 26:14).

WORLD

Whenever your eye lands on a list, whenever a phrase is repeated again and again, start counting. You'll often find a hint of Genesis 1 lurking in unexpected places.

Sevenfold patterns aren't mere literary devices. They describe God's characteristic way of working in the world. As we sense the rhythms of Scripture's sevens, we learn to sense the rhythm of our lives and the rhythms of the life of the world. Spiritual readers gain a good sense of rhythm and learn to read the rhythms of world.

There and Back Again

Sevenfold plots, lists, and speeches are common in Scripture. So are chiasms. A "chiasm" is a way of organizing a text, whether a story, a speech, a letter, or a series of visions. In a chiastic text, the second half of the text repeats the first half in reverse order. Jesus uses chiasms with some frequency:

Sabbath
    was made for man
    not man
for Sabbath (Mark 2:27).

Or,

Many who are first
    shall be last;
    and the last
first (Matt 19:30).

That last one is especially neat, since the form exactly imitates the substance. Jesus says those who are first (Jews, leaders) will enter the kingdom last. In the course of the sentence, "last" and "first" trade places, which is *just* what Jesus is talking about.

Larger sections of Scripture are arranged in chiastic form. As many have noted, the flood is a large concentric text, centered on "Yahweh remembered Noah":

>   A. Violence in God's creation (6:11-12)
>   B. First divine address: resolution to destroy (6:13-22)
>   C. Second divine address: command to enter the ark (7:1-10)
>   D. Beginning of the flood (7:11-16)
>   E. The rising flood waters (7:17-24)
>   GOD'S REMEMBRANCE OF NOAH
>   E'. The receding flood waters (8:1-5)
>   D'. The drying of the earth (8:6-14)
>   C'. Third divine address: command to leave the ark (8:15-19)
>   B'. God's resolution to preserve order (8:20-22)
>   A'. Fourth divine address: covenant blessing and peace (9:1-17)

Chiasms may seem odd and exotic, but they're very common in ancient literature. Every ancient rhetorical text includes a section on the use of chiasmus. But their frequency in Scripture suggests something more is going on. Chiasms aren't arbitrary ways of organizing texts. The chiastic pattern tells us something profound about reality.

Chiasms are "there-and-back-again" patterns. The text moves out, or "up," to a climax and then returns back home. Along the way, things change. The end is never exactly like the beginning. The shire isn't the same shire when Bilbo returns. But there is a feeling of return. The whole Bible is a "there-and-back-again" story. God creates a world in 6 + 1 days and sets Adam in Eden. Adam seizes forbidden fruit and is driven from the garden out into the howling waste. Israel's history moves toward a crux, a literal crux: the cross of Jesus, the turning point of history.

From there, history runs in reverse: People estranged

from God are made His table companions. The Spirit of Jesus gathers divided nations into one body. Lands turn fruitful; deserts become gardens. The world begins to mature toward the new Jerusalem until the heavenly city comes to rest on earth, a great garden city, better than the beginning—a city that is and is not Paradise restored.

Thomas Aquinas was right: Everything is encompassed by a movement of *exitus* and *reditus*, of going-out from God in creation and return to God in new creation. The Bible is full of chiasms because creation moves in a great chiasm.

Conclusion

Nothing in Scripture is "merely literary." *Everything*, down to the design of a passage and the metaphors used, is instructive, designed to train us for every good work. Chiasms aren't mere literary devices either. They mimic the shape of history and show that every episode follows the contours of the whole. Spiritual readers pay attention to every dimension of the poetry because we know every detail matters, even the least of these.

Solomon knew a lot about plants, stars, and animals. But we shouldn't think of him as a zoologist or botanist or astronomer. The Bible mainly teaches us to think *with* plants and animals. We think with the lowliest creatures about the "highest" things. The Bible is an animal story about the serpent's temptation and Jesus the sacrificial Lamb, who ascends as the Lion of Judah to send the dove of the Spirit to hover over the world and form it into a new creation. It's a tale of trees, a star story, a treasure hunt, a fishing expedition, and a human story of mountains, cities, deserts, and adventures.

Spiritual readers learn to engage with the world through the Bible so that every thing and every moment becomes a gateway for communion with the Creator. God gave the world to Adam as food. As the Bible heals us, as we become strong on its solid food, our eyes are dazzled by a continuous feast of glory.

As Spiritual readers, our senses are trained to use created things, interpreted through Scripture, to make sense of the world and our place in it. Do you know some bramble bushes? Maybe you go to church with some. Are your co-workers snakes or jackals? Better study Scripture to learn how to battle them. Is your pastor a lion? I hope so. Are tyrants and wicked shepherds plotting together against the faithful? Read Revelation to anticipate the rest of the story. Are you stuck between Pharaoh's armies and the sea? Wait for it. Wait for the wind that will make a path of dry land.

As we learn the structural forms and plot patterns of the Bible, as we learn to engage history through the Bible, we gain a sense of where we are in the story. Is this a time of uprooting or planting, of breaking or building? Is it a time to gather or to scatter, to embrace or refrain? As we learn the Bible's recurring patterns, we learn to dance in rhythm with the world because the rhythm of the Word is the rhythm of the world.

3 ADAM

Jesus stretched out His hand and touched him.
Matthew 8:3

Jesus is Adam.

That is one of the most obvious types in the Bible. Paul's overview of history has three main characters: Adam, Moses, and Jesus (Rom 5:12-21). Paul mainly compares and contrasts the first and Last. Because of one man's sin, death and sin enter the world and spread. Because of Jesus' one act of righteousness, life and righteousness triumph. Through one man's disobedience, many are made sinners. By one man's obedience, many are made righteous. Jesus undoes the doings of the first Adam.

Paul also appeals to the Adam-Christ connection when he teaches on the resurrection. Here Paul doesn't contrast unrighteous Adam with righteous Jesus. He contrasts *created* Adam with new-created Jesus. Adam has a natural body, made "from the earth, earthy." The "second man" is from heaven. Jesus doesn't become "a living soul" but a "life-giving Spirit." At the last day, that transformation will happen to us. For now, we bear the natural image of the earthly man. At the resurrection, we will bear the image of the heavenly (1 Cor 15:45-49). Our present perishable, shameful, weak, natural body is sown as a seed so that an imperishable, glorious, powerful, spiritual body can sprout (1 Cor 15:42-44).

Though the Gospels rarely mention Adam, they're pervaded by the same Adam typology. Jesus calls himself "Son of Man" over seventy times (e.g., Matt 8:20; Mark 2:10; Luke 5:24; John 1:51). "What is man," Psalm 8 asks, "or the son of man?" The Psalmist answers by paraphrasing Genesis 1: God crowns the son of man with glory and majesty and gives him rule over the works of His hands—sheep, oxen, and beasts, birds and fish (Psa 8:5-6). The "Son of Man" is "Son of Adam."

In a vision, Daniel sees "one like a son of man" ascending to the Ancient of Days to receive rule, dominion, and a kingdom (Dan 7:9-14). That dominion once belonged to beasts—a winged lion, a lopsided bear, a winged leopard, and an indescribably ferocious monster (Babylon, Persia, Greece, and Rome). The Son of Man recovers the authority of Adam. Jesus the Son of Man is Daniel's beast-tamer.

Jesus' life parallels and inverts Adam's. He's born outside normal lines of descent, born of a virgin as Adam was born from untilled, virgin earth (Matt 1:23, 25). He's tempted by Satan to turn stones into bread. Jesus refuses, though He is fasting in the wilderness (Matt 4:1-11). Unlike Adam, He doesn't break the fast. Jesus' miracles undo the curse. With a touch or a word, He cleanses leprosy, straightens limbs, purges impurities, raises the dead. He restores glory to the deformed children of Adam. He wears a crown of cursed thorns to die on a tree (Gen 3:18) and suffers outside the gate, exiled from Eden (Gen 3:24). At his trial, Pilate presents Jesus to the mobs: "Behold the man" (John 19:5). Behold *man*. Behold Adam, cursed Adam, shamed Adam, soon-to-be new Adam, risen in glory.

Adam in Eden

Jesus is Adam. That's obvious. But it can be misunderstood. It's misunderstood if we misconstrue Adam's original situation.

Christians sometimes assume Adam's situation is static. He's in Paradise with everything he needs. Why would he want to go anywhere else? We might think Eden is a lost ideal to which we will someday return. Salvation is a return to the beginning. Adam falls into a world of change and time. Salvation means rescue from time and change.

That's *all* wrong. Adam's not supposed to stay in Paradise. God commands Adam to be fruitful, multiply, and fill the earth (Gen 1:26-28). He can't do that if he stays in Eden. God commands him to subdue the earth and rule it (Gen 1:28). He can't do that by staying in Eden either. He's supposed to make the rest of the world *like* Paradise.

Adam's descendants share Adam's original vocation. We people the planet. We discover creation's powers and potentials, turn metals into flying machines and self-driving cars, plough and plant to make the land productive, carve stone into sculpture and organize sounds into symphonies, explore the depths of the sea and heights of the tallest mountains and hurtle out toward distant galaxies, tend forests and care for animals so our great-great-grandchildren can delight in the dazzling variety of God's creation.

God makes the world glorious. Creation *is* glory, a created radiance of the glory of God. Everything in creation reveals a facet of His beauty. Adam is God's agent to make it *more* glorious.

In this, Adam mimics his Creator. Even at the beginning, the world isn't changeless. Each day during the creation week, God remodels the world to make it better. Darkness isn't great, so He calls light into existence and calls it "good." Day 2 dawns, and He's busy moving waters up and setting a firmament. As soon as

Day 3 comes, He's not satisfied with what He's done, so He divides the waters below and summons the land to produce plants. That's good, but only until Day 4, when He does something brand new yet again. A lighted world is glorious. A lighted world with waters above and below is more glorious. A lighted world with heaven, earth, and sea is more glorious still. But a filled world is better than an empty one, so He spends the second half of the creation week filling it.

By the time Yahweh sits back to take His Sabbath delight, creation is more beautiful than ever. But this process doesn't end on the first Sabbath. God hasn't stopped nudging the world from glory to glory. *Every* day from Day 1 to this very moment brings something new.

As the image of God, Adam exists to remodel and fill, to keep the world moving from glory to glory. Our destiny is *not* a return to Eden. Our final home will be a *city*, adorned with the treasures of the nations (Rev 21:1—22:5). Paul says the same in 1 Corinthians 15:44: "If there is a natural body, there is a spiritual body." He doesn't say, "If there is a *sinful* body, there's a spiritual body." A Spiritual body doesn't merely reverse the effects of sin. A Spiritual body is a glorification of creation. Creation is designed to be glorified by Adam and his children. Glory is where creation is heading, whether or not Adam sinned. As children of Adam, we take and touch the world, break it down, and reassemble it to increase the voltage of its glory.

Along with the rest of creation, Adam and his children are created to be glorified. Human beings glorify and are glorified in glorifying. Human progress from glory to glory is one of the main threads of biblical history. James Jordan has said the Bible tells a triple story:

- It's a story of *sin and redemption*. God creates Adam and Eve. They sin and are condemned to death. God sends Jesus to

rescue humanity from sin and death and restore us to communion with Him.
- It's a story of *holy war*. God creates Adam and Eve. God permits a serpent to tempt Eve. Adam is supposed to crush the serpent's head right then and there, but fails. History is God's centuries-long war against Satan and his seed. Jesus comes as the Seed of the Woman to conquer the serpent and to give us power to trample Satan underfoot.
- It's a story of *maturation*. God creates Adam and Eve as children. They serve in the garden, but they're supposed to grow up into king and queen, prophet and prophetess. Their sin interrupts and impedes their education. Under the Old Covenant, God cares for Israel as a young child, training him toward adulthood. Jesus is the mature man and restores us to the path of maturity, so we and the world grow from glory to glory.

Each storyline hinges on the two Adams. The first Adam sins, but the Last Adam brings redemption. The first Adam is defeated by the serpent, but the Last Adam crushes his head. The first Adam is an infant, naked as a newborn. The Last Adam is the first fully mature man.

Many Christians get stuck on the first storyline: The Bible is "redemptive history." That's true but too narrow. We'll miss much of what the Bible is about—and much of its practical force—if we don't recognize it's also a story of war and a history of the maturation of humanity. Spiritual readers discern the multiple layers of biblical history.

Paul doesn't limit himself to "redemptive history." There's an interesting twist in Romans 5. He starts verse 17 with "if by the transgression of the one, death reigned through the one." We expect him to end the sentence with something like "so, by the righteousness of the one, life reigns through the one." We expect a transition from death into life.

That's *not* what he says, not exactly. The end of the sentence is "much more those who receive the abundance of grace and of the gift of righteousness will reign in life through the One, Jesus Christ." The reign of death hasn't given way to the reign of life. Paul doesn't even say the reign of Adamic sin has given way to the reign of Jesus. Rather, the reign of death has been overcome by the reign of those who receive grace and righteousness. The reign of death is succeeded by the reign in life of the justified. God overturns the regime of Adam by putting the saints on thrones.

This fits snugly in his presentation of the gospel in Romans. Paul *doesn't* summarize the gospel as "justification by grace through faith." He summarizes the gospel as a royal announcement: It's good news "concerning His Son, who was born of the seed of David according to the flesh" and "declared Son of God with power by the resurrection from the dead." The aim of the gospel is "to bring about the obedience of faith among the Gentiles, for His name's sake" (Rom 1:1-4).

Paul's gospel isn't just about rescue from sin. It's not only about forgiveness or our right standing with God. All of that fits into a larger, cosmic proclamation. The gospel is the good news that King Jesus now reigns, with the corollary good news that we reign with Him.

We can fill out the story of maturation by thinking about priests, kings, and prophets. Adam is placed in the garden to "guard" (Heb. *shamar*) and "serve" it (Heb. *'abad*) (Gen 2:15). "Serve and guard" is *sanctuary* terminology. Aaron is ordained to carry out the *'abodah* (service) of the sanctuary (Num 18:6-7). Priests are guardians. They *shamar* their priesthood (Num 3:8) and do "guard duty" (*mismeret*, from *shamar*) at the tabernacle (Num 3:31-32, 38).

In nearly every instance, the terms "serve and guard" apply to Levites. Levites and priests aren't identical. Aaron is from the tribe of Levi, but only his family serves as priests. The rest of the tribe helps the priests by doing the service (*'abodah*) of the sanctuary. Levites do guard duty (Num 1:53; 3:7-8, 28) and are authorized to kill intruders (Num 1:51; 3:10). Placed in the garden to "serve and guard," Adam is a junior-level priest, a "Levite" to the chief priest of the garden, the Angel of Yahweh.

Adam isn't supposed to remain a junior priest forever. He's to grow up into full priesthood and into kingship. That's what the two trees represent. The first tree, the tree of life, is freely available. Adam can eat of it any time, without restriction. He doesn't have to earn or merit life. Life—both biological life and life with God—is a gift given from the beginning, a gift to newborn Adam.

The other tree represents "knowledge of good and evil" (Gen 2:9, 17). In the Bible, this phrase refers to royal insight and the wisdom to discern and judge (2 Sam 14:17; 1 Kgs 3:9). We acquire royal discernment by experience as our senses are trained by life and by attention to the Word of God. The fruit of the tree of knowledge is "solid food" reserved "for the mature" (Heb 5:14). Adam can't eat it yet because he hasn't been trained. Someday, after he's fought his battles and gained wisdom by subduing and ruling the earth, after his senses have been trained by the Word of God, his kingly status would be sealed by a feast at the royal tree. After passing the "taste not, touch not" test, Adam would be crowned and enthroned at his Father's right hand. The world would be given into his hands.

Instead, Adam seizes a royal privilege before the Lord gives it to him. He's not wrong to want knowledge of good and evil. He's not wrong to want his eyes opened. He's wrong to assume he's ready. He sins because he loses faith in his Father and becomes impatient. He lays hands on God's royal treasure before God is ready to open the treasure chamber. He just can't wait to be king.

Adam is to mature from priest to king and then to prophet. A prophet is a member of Yahweh's council (Jer 23:18-22) who overhears the decisions of Yahweh's court and delivers them to the people (1 Kgs 22). A prophet is a trusted advisor with the prestige to talk back to God (Amos 7:1-9). God discloses His plans to prophets and listens to their counsel.

From priest to king to prophet: That is the trajectory of humanity's growth toward adulthood. It's the trajectory of the Bible. During the Mosaic era, Israel is a priestly nation (Exod 19:6) with Aaron the High Priest as chief leader. The Mosaic order collapses at the end of the period of judges, and Samuel anoints Saul and David as kings. The priestly nation becomes a kingdom. The Davidic order also ends in disaster when the Assyrians and Babylonians invade and conquer the divided kingdom. Prophets already appear in the time of kings, but they take on a higher profile just before, during, and after the exile. Israel is a microcosm of humanity, encapsulating the maturation of the race until the Messiah arrives, who is priest, king, and prophet in one Man.

At many levels, our lives have the same shape. To play the cello, you first have to submit to strict disciplines (like a priest), focusing on how you bend your fingers, where to touch the strings, how to hold the bow. By practice, you gain mastery (king). Eventually, you forget your fingers and the bow because you now integrate and embody the disciplines. Bow and cello feel like extensions of your body. Now you can *play*. Once you're a master, you can become a teacher (prophet), imposing disciplines on young students until they become kings of the strings. Through these stages, your senses are trained until you can tell the difference between excellence and incompetence. Through practice, you develop a touch for the instrument.

Golfers and knitters, poets and painters, businessmen and accountants, mothers and midwives, pastors and politicians mature through a similar sequence. A well-formed life moves through these phases. Early on, we're priestly servants, children under discipline gaining skills, following instructions, obeying the rules. After the crisis of early adulthood, we emerge as kings, building families, answering the calls of vocations, gaining influence, issuing rather than obeying commands, passing judgments. Many see their achievements collapse in mid-life, but they come to new life with deeper, calmer wisdom, the ancient wisdom of prophets, who live on to advise priests and kings. As you read your experience through the lens of God's Word, you get in touch with the world.

Adam is a child. The Last Adam is the fully-formed adult. Every character of the Bible is somewhere between the first and Last, somewhere between first and final glory. So are each of us, stretched out between creation and new Jerusalem. For the story of the first and Last Adams is also *our* story, and we find our bearings by remembering our beginning and anticipating our end. Reading Scripture trains our senses to read our lives.

Many Adams

Jesus is Adam. That can be misunderstood. It's misunderstood when we miss the force of Paul's term in 1 Corinthians 15:45: Jesus is indeed the "second man" (1 Cor 15:47). But He's described as the "*last* Adam" (1 Cor 15:45; *eschatos*). Jesus isn't just second. He's the *final* Adam. There are *many* Adams between Adam and Jesus.

The whole story of the Bible stretches out between the first and the Last Adam, but a chain of Adams links the two. Some mimic the first Adam in his sin, some anticipate the righteousness of the Last Adam, and some do each at different moments. Each man in Scripture needs to be seen bifocally through the double lens of the first and Last Adam.

Noah is an Adam. He lives in the tenth generation from Adam (Gen 5:1-32). During his life, the Lord de-creates the world, turning it back to the watery void that preceded His creative word (Gen 7:17-24). Noah is the father of the new humanity that emerges from that "formless void." Despite man's propensity to evil, Yahweh doesn't give up on His original plan. He commands Noah to be fruitful and multiply (Gen 9:1) and gives him dominion over the animals as He did with Adam (Gen 9:2). After Noah emerges from the ark, the book of Beginnings revs up with more genealogies, showing that the race of Adam continues through the new Adam.

Abraham is also an Adam. After Yahweh scatters the nations from Shinar, He starts to form a new, united humanity within the old, divided humanity. He promises to make Abraham fruitful and to multiply him—that is, He promises to fulfill the vocation of Adam through Abraham's seed (Gen 17:20). Yahweh promises dominion. Abraham doesn't settle in the land himself, but the land is given to his descendants. Kings will be born from him (Gen 17:6, 16). Together, the promises of land and seed are a promise of a new Eden. Once the seed of Abraham is planted in the land, Yahweh promises to make them grow until the land becomes a garden, a fertile field.

"How can I know?" Abraham asks. Yahweh answers by telling him to perform a ritual (Gen 15). Abraham kills and divides several animals and lays the parts side-by-side to make a pathway between. Yahweh puts Abraham into a deep sleep (Heb. *tardemah*) and then passes through the pieces, flaming like a torch (Gen 15:12-21). Only one other man in Genesis falls into a "deep sleep"—Adam, when Yahweh takes a rib to build a woman (Gen 2:21-22). Adam goes into a deep sleep to receive the gift of a bride. Abraham goes into a deep sleep to receive the promised gift of land. Both foreshadow the Last Adam, who enters the sleep of death in order to receive a bride and inherit the ends of the earth.

Like Adam, Abraham speaks with his wife just after he wakes up. Sarah tells Abraham to father a son with her maidservant

Hagar (Gen 16:2). Abraham does it: He "listened to the voice of Sarai" (Gen 16:2), just as Adam "listened to the voice of his wife" and took the forbidden fruit (Gen 3:17). By contrast, Abraham is a model of faith and faithfulness, an obedient Adam. With Hagar, he repeats the fall and seizes the fruit of the promise before God's time.

Abraham is Adam in a deeper, more subtle sense. As the first man, Adam represents the human race. Whatever he does affects everyone who comes after. He's tossed from Eden, and so are his children and grandchildren. He's a representative "head" of the human race. Abraham plays the same role in relation to Israel. Yahweh loves Israel for the sake of Abraham, Isaac, and Jacob (Deut 4:37; 7:7-11). The father's actions determine the destiny of his children.

Because he's head, Abraham's entire life story anticipates the history of Israel. He's called from Ur into the land but soon finds the land is barren (Gen 12:10). Famine drives him to Egypt, where Pharaoh tries to seize Sarai until Yahweh touches him with plagues (Gen 12:17-18). Pharaoh sends Abraham out enriched (Gen 12:16); Abraham plunders Egypt. Once he's back in the land, Abraham gets sucked into a war that leaves him with military supremacy in the land (Gen 13-14).

In nearly every particular, Abraham's story matches Israel's. Famine? Check (Gen 41:50-57). Move to Egypt? Check (Gen 47:1-19). Oppressive Pharaoh? Check (Exod 1-2). Plagues? *Ten* checks (Exod 7-12). Departure with plunder? Check (Exod 12:36). Conquest of the land, including a battle with five kings? Check (Josh 10:1-15).

Abraham is a new Adam, *and* Abraham is a proto-Israel. Let's put these two facts into a petri dish and see what grows. I expect this: If Abraham is an Adam and if Abraham is the father of Israel, then Israel is a new Adamic people. The history of the seventy nations (Gen 10) is played out in miniature within Israel, which is also a collection of seventy (Gen 46:27). Spiritual readers discern the layers of Abraham's life as he embodies both Adam and Israel.

Moses is another good example of how the Bible "layers" Adams on top of each other. On the face of it, Moses is a new Noah:

- His "basket" is an "ark" (Exod 2:3, 5). The Hebrew word tebah is the same one used for Noah's ark (Gen 6:14-16).
- The waters of the Nile are waters of death (Exod 1:22), as are the waters of the flood. Moses, like Noah, passes safely through, untouched by Pharaoh, saved by baptism.
- Moses later leads a great company through deadly waters, a much larger company than the eight persons in Noah's ark.
- Moses leads Israel through the waters to a mountain. Sinai is a new Ararat (cf. Gen 8:4). The human race restarts from Ararat, and the new humanity of Israel cuts covenant at Sinai.
- At the foot of Sinai, Moses builds the tabernacle—Eden in tent form (see ch. 5)—just as Noah planted a vineyard after the flood.
- As soon as the tabernacle is finished, Aaron's sons defile it with strange fire (Lev 10) as Ham sinned and was cursed at Noah's vineyard (Gen 9:20-27).

Moses is a new Noah. Noah is a new Adam. Therefore, Moses is, indirectly, also another Adam. He's head of a nation, like Adam and Abraham. He has a priestly role, and he rules. Like Adam, Moses stands before the face of God, converses with Yahweh mouth-to-mouth (Num 12:6-8), and comes away "horned" with glory (Exod 34:29-34). To catch the full meaning of Moses' work, we need to see traces of Noah, which are refractions of Adam.

And Moses points to Jesus, the Greater Moses. Infant Jesus is saved from a murderous tyrant (Matt 2:1-12), passes through the Jordan as through the sea (Matt 3:13-17), endures trials in the wilderness (Matt 4:1-11), teaches Torah from a mountain (Matt 5—7), leads an exodus from the old world into a new creation (Luke 9:31), and ascends into the cloud of glory (Acts 1:6-11).

Moses' brother Aaron is an Adam too. The tabernacle is a new garden (see chapter 5), and Aaron and his sons are priestly Adams. Aaron draws near to Yahweh to stand and serve in His presence, something no man has done since Adam was driven from Eden. Priests eat the food of the sanctuary, the showbread on the golden table (Lev 24:5-16), as Adam was given the fruit of the tree of life. Aaron cares for the lampstand, a stylized golden tree, a burning bush (Lev 24:1-4), as Adam tended the trees of the garden. Adam was created a junior priest. Under the Mosaic law, Aaron and his descendants are restored to priestly service until Jesus comes as a better priest in the order of Melchizedek (Heb 7).

King David sees himself as an Adam. Yahweh's promise to David's dynasty goes beyond David's imagination. "Who am I, Lord God, and what is my house, that Thou hast brought me this far?" (1 Chr 17:16), David asks in astonishment. Yahweh's promise is not merely about David's immediate descendants but about "the distance" (1 Chr 17:17). And Yahweh's promise to David doesn't pertain only to Israel. It involves all humanity. Yahweh treats David as "a man of high degree" (1 Chr 17:17). The word for "man" is *'adam*, and the verb is *'alah*, "ascend." Yahweh regards David as "an Adam ascended" (1 Chr 17:17). By his elevation to kingship, to sonship, to membership in Yahweh's own household and family, David is a new Adam. Through David, Yahweh pledges to bring humanity as a whole to royal splendor and authority.

Like Saul, who preceded him as king (cf. 1 Sam 13—15), David is also an Adam in the negative sense. Chosen from his brothers, raised to kingship, granted victory after victory over his enemies, he risks it all for a one-night stand with a beautiful woman (2 Sam 11—12). Repeating the fall, David sees Bathsheba is good, takes, and tastes her. To cover his crime, he becomes a Cain and kills her husband. Over the following years, his house and kingdom are wracked by the incestuous passion of Amnon for his sister Tamar, Absalom's murder of Amnon, Absalom's rebellion, and the rebellion of Sheba. David enjoys a moment of Edenic glory but loses it on one night. 'Tis like another fall of man.

As son of David, Solomon is Adam in royal mode. He rules a great people, fulfilling Adam's calling to take dominion of the earth. Kings come to hear his wisdom. He knows about plants and trees, animals, birds, creeping things, and fish (1 Kgs 4:33; cf. Gen 1:28).

Like his father, Solomon is a fallen Adam. His wisdom doesn't keep him from the folly of idolatry. In ancient Israel, kings are prohibited from multiplying gold, horses and chariots, and wives (Deut 17:16-17). Solomon breaks all the rules. He gathers horses and chariots, multiplies gold (1 Kgs 10:14-29), and, worst of all, marries many foreign women who turn his heart from Yahweh to idols (1 Kgs 11:1-13). David loses his kingdom temporarily because of his sin. Solomon's sins have more catastrophic results: Ten tribes embark on an exodus from the house of David (1 Kgs 12).

In the latter part of the Old Testament, many of the main characters are prophets: Elijah and Elisha in the northern kingdom of Israel, Isaiah and Jeremiah in the kingdom of Judah, Ezekiel and Daniel, exilic seers. Israel's prophets reach a stage of glory beyond the first Adam and anticipate the Last more precisely. Isaiah speaks obscure words to a deaf and blind people (Isa 6:8-13), as does Jesus (Matt 13:15). Jeremiah prophesies doom to the temple (Jer 7), as does Jesus (Matt 24). Jeremiah is attacked for telling the truth (Jer 38), like Jesus. Jesus' baptism recalls Ezekiel's vision of the glory chariot (Ezek 1; Luke 3:21-23), and Jesus the "Son of Man" fulfills the vision of Daniel.

None of these priests, kings, prophets, or heroes are identical to Adam. Each is unique. But each is modeled by some aspect of Adam, and each foreshadows some fold in the glory of the Last Adam.

ADAM

Improved Adams

Jesus is Adam. That may be misunderstood. We misunderstand when we fail to recognize there are many Adams. We misunderstand when we fail to see the *progression* from Adam to Adam. The many Adams are not merely repetitions of the first Adam. They're improvements. They're glorified Adams. God doesn't give up on His plan to educate the human race. Even in a world of sin, humanity matures from glory to glory. Before Jesus comes, Adams are trained by practice and God's word to discern good and evil.

Noah is a glorified Adam. Adam is allowed to eat plants (Gen 1:29-30), but Noah is given permission to eat flesh, though not blood (Gen 9:3-4). Noah is given royal authority to punish evildoers (Gen 9:5-7). Adam never does that. Noah builds an altar and offers the first "ascension offering" (Heb. *'olah*) in the Bible (Gen 8:20-22).[2] Yahweh plants a garden for the first Adam (Gen 2:8). Noah, a second Adam, plants his *own* vineyard and enjoys wine, beverage of kings (Gen 9:20-21; cf. Gen 40:1-15; Psa 75:8; Jer 25:12-29). Adam is a junior priest, destined to become king. Noah *is* a king.

Noah's superiority to Adam is evident in the most misunderstood episode of Noah's life. After he drinks wine, Noah uncovers himself in his tent. Ham sees him and tells his brothers, who discretely cover their father (Gen 9:21-23). Many Christians think Noah is at fault: Noah the drunkard, Noah the flasher. That's not how Noah sees it. He pronounces a curse on Ham's son, Canaan, and blesses Shem and Japheth for showing respect (Gen 9:25-27). Whatever is going on here, *Ham* is the one at fault, not Noah. Noah plays a *Godlike* role, pronouncing curses against sinners—*effective* curses (cmp. Gen 3:8-19). Adam is made in the image and likeness of God. Noah images God more fully.

---

[2] See *Theopolitan Liturgy*, 64.

THEOPOLITAN READING

Abraham, too, is a matured Adam. We don't know whether Adam actually ruled animals or men, but Abraham has large herds and flocks and enough servants to raise a fighting force of 318 men (Gen 14:14). Adam defies God, but Abraham continually worships God at altars he sets up throughout the land (Gen 12:7-8; 13:4, 18). Adam is impatient, touching and tasting the fruit before he is ready. Abraham shows some impatience, but mainly he trusts Yahweh to keep His promise even when it seems death has triumphed.

Abraham's and Sarah's fertility surpasses that of Adam and Eve. The original couple has children naturally, by the potency of flesh. The flesh of Abraham and Sarah is dead, but they trust Yahweh to raise new life from their dead bodies (Rom 4:16-21). When they receive their miracle child, Abraham willingly gives him back to Yahweh, trusting Him to raise Isaac from the altar as He raised him from Sarah's dead womb (Gen 22; cf. Heb 11:8-12). Abraham's life hints ahead to the resurrection life of the Last Adam, who gives His Spirit to bring the dead to life.

Abraham performs priestly tasks, building and worshiping at altars. He is also a "mighty prince" (Gen 23:6), ruling his household, conquering the land, taking dominion of animals. He's also a prophet (Gen 20:7), the first in Scripture. As prophet, he intercedes for Abimelech, whose house suffers a plague of barrenness after Abimelech seizes Sarah (Gen 20:2-6, 18), as he prays for Sodom (Gen 18:22-33).

Abraham's immediate descendants are also *improved* Adams. Both Isaac and Jacob own enormous flocks and herds (Gen 24:15; 26:14; 30:25-43), and Jacob has twelve sons and some daughters. They rule large households. Jacob is a "perfect" man (Gen 25:27) who overcomes the murderous hostility of his brother, Esau, and the manipulations of his father-in-law, Laban, in order to prosper. Joseph's suffering and glory point ahead to the Last Adam: Joseph's brothers hate and betray him; he is thrown into a pit and a prison but rises; he eventually becomes ruler of Egypt, second only to Pharaoh, and feeds bread to the world. Coming at the end of Genesis, Joseph partially overcomes the sin of Adam at the beginning of Genesis. Joseph is a sign that Yahweh will undo the first Adam's sin and send a greater Joseph, a Last Adam.

Genesis begins with three falls. Adam sins against God in the garden. His son Cain sins against his brother by killing him in the field (Gen 4:1-15). The sons of God, who are the descendants of Seth, intermarry with daughters of men, and their offspring fill the world with violence and wickedness (Gen 6:1-5). Adam is cast from the garden, Cain from the land, and in the flood the sons of God perish from the earth. Cain continues his father's assault on God by assaulting God's image. Adam is the original "son of God" (Luke 3:38), and the sons of God repeat his sin by seizing forbidden fruit: the daughters of men (female descendants of Cain). Cain and the sons of God are variations on an Adamic theme.

Abraham, Jacob, and Joseph invert each of these fallen Adams in turn. Abraham worships God and lives a life of patient faith: He turns Adam upside down. Jacob is an Abel who parries his brother's attacks and survives his assault: He upends Esau, a new Cain. Joseph resists the seductions of Potiphar's wife and brings life rather than death to the world: He's the true son of God. Abraham, Jacob, and Joseph are variations on a Last-Adamic theme.

Other Adams of the Old Testament are improvements on the first Adam. Despite sin, God remains faithful to His plan to glorify humanity. He's determined to train their senses so they become His mature children, sharing His reign over creation.

As a new Noah, Moses is a glorified Adam. He's not merely a priest serving in the garden; he's a prophetic architect. Moses "dies and rises" twice: in the Nile and at the Red Sea.

Like Isaac, he's a *risen* Adam. Moses' powers are nearly God-like. He is God to Pharaoh, while Aaron is his prophet (Exod 7:1). He performs potent signs and wonders in Egypt and the wilderness. With a touch of his rod, he brings death and life. In the beginning, Yahweh directly speaks the world into existence. He speaks seven times to lay out the plans for the tabernacle (Exod 25-31; see ch. 2), but *Moses* is the creative agent who actually makes the tabernacle. Hearing Yahweh's Word, gripped by the Word, Moses assumes some of the power of the Word. When his face shines with glory, Moses looks a lot like Yahweh.

Saul starts as an improved Adam, defeating the serpent-king Nahash (1 Sam 11:1-15; *nahash* means "serpent"). Instead Saul repeats the sins of Adam (by being impatient in worship; 1 Sam 13), Cain (by trying to kill his son Jonathan; 1 Sam 14), and the sons of God (by allying with Agag the Amalekite king; 1 Sam 15).

David sins too, but he also surpasses the first Adam. Adam is placed in a garden. David conquers and builds a city (2 Sam 5:1-12). David has discernment like an "angel of God," knowing good and evil (2 Sam 14:17), and Solomon, too, is given "knowledge of good and evil" (1 Kgs 3:6-15). It's as if they've eaten the fruit of Eden's second tree. Adam is placed in a garden sanctuary; like Noah and Moses, Solomon builds himself a garden. Like Noah and Moses, David and Samuel are human "gods."

Israel's prophets are greater Adams. Adam never attains to prophetic stature. He never performs miracles like Elijah and Elisha, never speaks words to uproot and plant like Jeremiah, is never (so far as we know) caught up, like Ezekiel, into the glory to see Yahweh's throne. Each prophet is a sign that the Creator's plan to mature the human race is going forward. He continues to move the world from glory to glory.

That series of new-and-improved Adams comes to its climax in Jesus. He's the "last" Adam. That doesn't just mean His is the last name on a list of Adams. It means He's everything Adam is created to be. Jesus is a fully-human human, the first of His kind. As the *eschatos* Adam, He's head of a new humanity, of fully-human men and women. His touch heals broken humanity so we can finish Adam's work, so we can touch, take, and glorify creation.

Each Adam foreshadows the Last. Jesus is not only Last Adam but also a greater Noah, a son of Abraham, a new Moses, a priest better than Aaron, a conqueror like Joshua, a strongman like Gideon and a riddling Samson, a prophet like Samuel and Elisha and Jeremiah, a scribe of the law like Ezra, and a builder of cities like Nehemiah. Jesus sums up everything that went before. All Adams accumulate and cluster around Jesus. Every Adam is a piece of the mosaic. When assembled, they reveal the beautiful face of the heavenly King.

But they're accumulating even before Jesus arrives. Every new Adam not only builds on the first Adam but builds on others. Abraham isn't simply a new Adam; he's also a new Noah. Moses is a new Noah and a new Adam and points ahead to Samuel, David, and Elijah. Joshua is a conquering Adam and, as servant of and successor to Moses, anticipates the work of Elisha. Every prophet is not only a matured Adam but an improvisation on the great prophet, Moses.

To read well, we need to discern how *every* previous Adam is layered like Jesus. Each sums up everything that comes before *Him*, even as each anticipates the full-formed *eschatos* Adam.

In the Last Adam

Jesus is raised above all rule and authority and power and dominion. He's above every name and fills all things (Eph 1:21-23). He has completed the Adamic vocation to fill and rule.

Jesus *will* complete Adam's vocation in and through us,

in concrete, historical reality. We are seated with Jesus in heavenly places (Eph 2:6). Not, "We *will* rule," though we shall. We rule *now*. Not, "We rule *spiritually*," which is to say, not *really*. No, we *really* rule. We rule all things. All things are yours. Everything is your servant. Everything belongs to Christ, and you are members of Christ's body. You are heirs of the world (1 Cor 3:21-22). Everything you touch belongs to you because it belongs to the Last Adam, and you are in Him. Everything you touch is sanctified by the Word and prayer (1 Tim 4:4-5). Whatever's holy becomes God's possession and ours because He shares all He has—Himself above all.

We sometimes read the Bible's drama of the first and Last Adam as something that takes place *outside* of us, as if we're spectators. Adam messes everything up. Lots of Adams come and go. Jesus puts everything back together. Curtain falls. A great show.

But an Adam is a representative head of a people. Adam is the head of the whole human race. Jesus is the Last Adam, head of all things for the church. United to Christ, we are the new humanity. The whole history of the world comes to its climax in Jesus, and because we're in Jesus, it comes to a climax *in us*, His church.

All the Adams reach fulfillment in the *totus Christ*, the *whole* Christ, who is both head and body. The *eschatos* world has arrived in the *eschatos* Adam, and we are His. It doesn't arrive in some invisible, "spiritual" form. The end arrives in communities of real men and women and children. It arrives in our rites of baptism, in our meals of bread and wine, in our prayers and praise, in the communion we have with one another in Christ, in our service for the life of the world. We are the last men, the last women, the people of the future. The end arrives *in us*.

All previous Adams accumulate and cluster around *us*. In Christ, we are Noah, navigating the ark of the church through stormy waters. In Christ, we are children of Abraham, sons and daughters born of the Spirit. In Christ, we are Israel-Jacob, wrestling with God and man and limping in triumph toward the promised land. In Christ, we are Moses, passing through the sea, enduring the howling wilderness, hearing and teaching the Word of God. In Christ, we are kings in the line of David, sons of the prophets who receive the Spirit to see visions and dream dreams. In Christ, we have matured, our senses trained to discern good and evil. The mosaic doesn't just picture the head. It's a full-length, whole-body portrait. *We* are that body.

Each Adam is an archetype that helps us make sense of our lives and our place in history. We follow the examples of these Adams because we are disciples of the Last Adam, in whom all types cohere. Is the world filled with violence and evil? Are the storm clouds gathering for a global flood? Be Noah in the greater Noah; build the ark and plan your future vineyard. Do you cry out under the heavy hand of a Pharaoh? Is a tyrant hunting you and your children? Be Moses in the greater Moses; deflect Pharaoh's hand until you can march out of Egypt. Has the Lord graciously set the faithful on thrones? Be David, doing justice and righteousness; rule with Solomonic wisdom by the Spirit of the One greater than Solomon. Are you in exile? Have you been forbidden to pray? Dare to be a Daniel.

This is what the *gospel* is all about. Jesus comes not merely to rescue us from sin, certainly *not* to rescue us from the world. Jesus *doesn't* come as the Last Adam to cancel the original Adamic task of ruling and filling. The Last Adam comes to accomplish the vocation of the first. In Him, we are priestly servants, royal judges, prophetic advisors. In Him, we're fruitful to fill the earth. In Him, we subdue and rule the earth, glorifying the glorious creation until it is nothing but the heavenly city of God. In Him, we've grown up.

"Adam and Christ" is the substructure of the gospel. But we need to get it right. Not, "Jesus saves, and *in addition*

Jesus is King." Rather, Jesus saves *as* king. Salvation *is* Jesus becoming king and *sharing* His kingship, His new-Adamic reign in life. In Him, we take up the book and find *our* stories in His. In Him, we take the world until it's transfigured according to the pattern of the book.

4   EVE

My perfume gave forth its fragrance.
Song of Songs 1:12

The creation of Eve is startlingly novel. Nothing else remotely like it happens in the creation account. Nothing.

It's startling because it's God's response to something that's "not good" (Gen 2:18). Yahweh repeatedly declares the creation good—light is good, the division of earth's waters is good, plants are good, fish and birds are good, animals are good, *everything* is good. Then suddenly, "It's not good for the man to be alone." As the kids say, "Bam!"

It's startling, too, because of the way Yahweh makes the woman. When Yahweh wants light, He orders light, and light shines. When He wants plants, He talks to the earth and tells it to be fruitful (Gen 1:11-12). When He wants fish and birds, He says, "let the waters team" and "let birds fly on the face of the firmament" (Gen 1:20-22). He summons land animals from the earth with a word (Gen 1:24-25).

Adam's creation is different. Yahweh doesn't speak from a distance but digs in the clay, forming the *'adam* from the *'adamah*, the human from the humus. He makes Adam a living soul with a kiss of life (Gen 2:7). With Adam, Yahweh takes a hands-on approach.

When Yahweh prepares a companion for Adam, we expect Him to do something similar. He could call a woman from the ground. He could mold her as He did Adam. Instead, He goes through an elaborate process. He puts Adam into a deep sleep, removes a rib, closes the flesh, and "builds" (Heb. *banah*) the woman from the rib (Gen 2:21-22). It's a startingly violent, intrusive way to make a woman.

Why? Why the sleep? Why the rib? Why the elaborate procedure?

We can come up with various answers. Eve is the first living being to come from another living being, the first soul "born" from a soul. She's born, as it were, from a male "womb." Or we might note the movement from one (Adam) to two (Adam and Eve) to one (flesh). Eve comes from Adam because she's going to return to Adam in a unity glorified by diversity. As many have pointed out, Eve is taken from Adam to symbolize the intimacy between husband and wife.

Almost universally, the church fathers interpret the passage as a type of Christ. Like everything else in Genesis—like everything else in the *Bible*—this account is about Jesus. Eve comes from Adam's side as a preview of the church's birth as the Bride of Jesus, given life by the water and blood that come from Jesus' side (John 19:34). The water signifies baptism, and the blood points to the wine of the Eucharist. The Bride is made by water and blood from the Bridegroom. Augustine pithily sums up the tradition: "Eve was born from the side of her sleeping spouse, and the Church was born from the dead Christ by the mystery of blood which gushed from his side" (*Contra Faustum*, 12.8).

We can press the point: Jesus is the temple who is torn down on the cross (John 2:19-22). When pierced, He becomes a source of living water, like the temple of Ezekiel (Ezek 47:1-12). Women are often associated with wells and water (Gen 21:19; 24:11; Exod 2:16-21; Prov 5:15; John 4:7-38). The flow of water from Jesus the temple *is* the "Eve" that comes from the cut in the Last Adam's flesh. It's the "stream" of children that come from the marriage of the Last Adam with His Bride.

You might regard these readings as fanciful. You might turn up your nose in disgust. If so, you need your senses trained. You need to learn to read in the Spirit. The church fathers make sense of Genesis 2.[3]

Let's think about Adam's deep sleep. The word isn't the normal one for sleep, and it's used only one other time in Genesis (Gen 15:12), when Yahweh confirms the covenant bond with Abraham. Abraham's deep sleep is part of a sacrificial, covenant-making procedure. Abraham is an Adam, who will be fruitful, multiply, fill, and rule the land through his royal descendants. We can infer this: The first Adam's deep sleep is also a covenant-making, sacrificial procedure. Through it, Yahweh forges a marital covenant between Adam and Eve.

The creation of Eve is the first sacrifice. When Israelites offer sacrifice, they bring an animal, kill it, divide it into pieces, and turn it to smoke on the altar. Sacrifice isn't over when the animal is killed. Through fire, the animal is glorified and ascends to Yahweh. Sacrifice is a movement through death to glorification. So, too, with Adam. He's put into a death-like sleep. He's divided into two pieces. When he wakes, he finds Eve, his "glory" (1 Cor 11:7). The creation of Eve is Adam's sacrificial passage through death to glory. For the woman is the glory of the man. Adam to Eve is the first step in the Bible's story of glorification.

Death-to-glory is just what's happening to Jesus at the cross.

---

[3] The next few paragraphs overlap with *Theopolitan Liturgy*, 51-55.

He doesn't go into deep sleep. He *dies*. His body is opened so that blood and water rush out. He dies so that He will be raised and will build a Bride through the work of His Spirit, in the water and in the blood.

The church fathers are right. They read in the Spirit. Their senses were trained, so they became kings of interpretation. Jesus *is* Adam. Eve *is* the church, formed from the side of the Last Adam.

Now that's a big deal. If the Bible is the story of the first and Last Adams, it's also the story of the first and Last Eves. It's the story of the first woman, made from the side of the first Adam. It's the story of the church, the *eschatos* Eve, formed from the cross and resurrection of the heavenly Adam. It's not just the story of God or the God-Man. It's the history of God-and-the-world, Jesus-with-His Bride.

This talk about Eve is liable to the same misunderstandings we noted when we talked about Jesus as Adam. We're immature readers if we jump from Adam to Jesus as if Jesus were no more than a second Adam. There are many Adams. We're also immature readers if we jump from Eve to the church. There are *many* Eves, and the church embodies all of them in one way or another. Each Eve is a piece of the mosaic. When it's completed, we find it's a wedding picture of a Bride, robed in white, prepared for her Husband.

Mother of the Living

Eve is a complex character. She's the bridal glory from Adam's side. As such, she enhances the glory of the garden. The Song of Songs is a poetic recovery of Edenic eroticism, portraying a love of mutual possession (SoS 2:16; 6:3; 7:10) fired by the flame of Yah (SoS 8:6-7). In the Song of Songs, the Bride is a watered garden (SoS 4:12-15) with flowers, trees, and fruit (SoS 2:1; 7:7-8).

Adam is commissioned to guard the garden. As soon as Eve is added, he guards her too.

The links between glory-bride and garden form the background for much of the feminine symbolism in Scripture. Solomon's temple has a "face" (1 Kgs 6:3), "ribs" (1 Kgs 6:5, 8), and "shoulders" (1 Kgs 7:39). The language makes it clear that already in the Old Testament, the temple is "humaniform."

Not merely "humaniform," but "*femino*-form." Yahweh God took a "rib" from Adam, and Solomon's temple is surrounded by "ribs." Yahweh God closed the flesh "underneath," the same word translated as "lowest" in 1 Kings 6:6. Yahweh God "built" (Gen 2:22; Heb. *banah*) a woman for Adam, and 1 Kings 6 uses the same verb repeatedly (vv. 1, 2, 5, 7, 9, etc.). Israel's sanctuaries are feminine buildings, which Yahweh the Bridegroom "enters" for Sabbath delight.

Solomon is a new and greater Adam. He knows good and evil (1 Kgs 3:9, 11-12). He "has dominion" over the land (1 Kgs 4:21, 24). He speaks of plants and categories of living souls (1 Kgs 4:33-34). In 1 Kings 6—7, Solomon shows himself a superior Adam again: In the beginning, Yahweh God builds a bride for Adam. Solomon, the greater Adam, builds a bride-house for Yahweh.

At the end of the Bible, the garden-temple-bride nexus reappears. New Jerusalem has cubic dimensions, like the Most Holy Place (Rev 21:16). Revelation adds another layer. New Jerusalem is a temple-*city* (Rev 21:2, 10) as well as a "Bride adorned for her husband" (Rev 21:12), gleaming with the glory of God (Rev 21:11). Her arrival brings the marriage supper of the Lamb to its consummation (Rev 19:9-10).

Eve is the first mother and, therefore, mother of all the living (Gen 3:20), as her name indicates: *chavvah*, "Eve," is a pun on *chay*, "life." As mother, Eve is essential to the vocation the Lord gives man as "male and female." Adam can't be fruitful and multiply and fill the earth on his own. Dominion isn't a *male* vocation.

THEOPOLITAN READING

I've used the phrase "Adamic vocation" earlier in this book, but that's not entirely accurate. It's a human vocation—Adam-*and*-Eve-ic. The world must be peopled, and that requires both fathers and mothers.

Eve, not Adam, receives the promise of a Seed who will crush the head of the serpent (Gen 3:15-16). The Lord places enmity between *Eve* and the serpent, and the Deliverer is described as *her* child, not Adam's. The *woman* fights the serpent by giving birth to the head-crushing Savior.

Eve is, of course, also the one who succumbs to Satan's temptation and, so, is a paradigm of the fallen woman. According to Paul, the serpent attempts to "seduce" Eve (2 Cor 11:1-3) so that her children will serve the serpent rather than the Creator. Eve rightly discerns the tree is good for food and has the power to make one wise. But she is deceived by the serpent (Gen 3:13; 1 Tim 2:14) into seizing and tasting the fruit before it's offered. She can't wait to be queen.

The fault is Adam's. God reveals the prohibition of the tree of knowledge directly to Adam, prior to Eve's creation (Gen 2:15-17). Adam is supposed to guard her from the serpent's assault. After all, he's "with her" during the temptation, cowed by the serpent or waiting to see what happens (Gen 3:8).

Eve is Bride and mother, sinner and, in a sense, savior, as the mother of the future serpent-crusher. Every woman of the Bible captures one or another aspect of Eve's person and history. And every woman in history lives between the first Eve and the Last, as every man is suspended between Adams. Spiritual readers sense the scent of Eve in the Bible's women.

Seductresses and Whores

Eves are often tempted or assaulted by serpentine figures. When Abraham takes Sarah to Egypt, Pharaoh tries to take her into his harem (Gen 12:14-15). Abimelech does the same (Gen 20:2). A later Pharaoh tries to stop Hebrew women from having male children. He's a serpent, who kills to prevent the birth of a seed who would crush Egypt's head (Exod 1:8-22).

John sees a woman in the sky, in labor to give birth to a son. Nearby, a dragon waits to devour the newborn child (Rev 12:1-4). It's a snapshot of the history of the Old Testament: Israel is the woman, enduring a centuries-long labor to give birth to the Messiah, always threatened by serpents who seek to devour. The Old Testament is a long birth story with many complications.

Eve is tempted. Other "Eves" *tempt*. Sarah encourages Abram to have a child with Hagar. As Adam "listened to his wife" and ate, so Abram "listened to his wife" and took his concubine (Gen 3:17; 16:2). Potiphar's wife is a hyped-up temptress who tries to seduce Joseph, strips his robe, leaves him naked and shamed, and accuses him of trying to rape her (Gen 39:6-18).

Lady Folly in Proverbs is another hyped-up Eve. She isn't deceived; she's a deceiver. She isn't seduced by the serpent; she seduces. Dressed like a harlot, boisterous and forward, she seizes a passing simpleton, kisses him, and lures him to a bed covered with Egyptian linens and spices. She promises a torrid night of love and freedom from detection because her husband is off on a business trip (Prov 7:10-20). She entices the fool with promises of stolen water and secret bread (Prov 9:15-17). Her victims are so naïve that they don't realize her house is a gateway to Sheol (Prov 7:22-23; 9:18). Eve herself isn't Lady Folly, but Lady Folly is a corrupted Eve, a prostituted bride.

Eve is the original model for prostituted Israel. At Sinai, Yahweh enters a marriage covenant with His people Israel. He rescues Zion, feeds and cares for her, clothes her with porpoise skin sandals, and puts a ring on her nose. Yet she turns from her Husband and chases every idol, every passing penis (Ezek 16:1-22; 23:1-49).

"You are a harlot with many lovers," Yahweh scolds Judah. She pollutes the land with idolatrous harlotry (Jer 3:1-5). As she is taken to exile, her nose, once adorned, will be cut off (Ezek 23:25). The jewel on her nose will be replaced with a hook as she's led like a beast to a strange land.

Some women in the Bible are actual seducers. Lot's daughters get him drunk and sleep with him so the human race will continue past the destruction of Sodom. Their sons, Moab and Ammon, are a persistent threat to Israel (Gen 19:30-38).

Some women look like seducers but prove otherwise. Tamar marries two sons of Judah, each of whom dies because of his wickedness. Judah is supposed to give her his youngest son, Shelah, so she can have an heir in Judah's line, but he delays. To secure her right, she dresses as a prostitute and sleeps with her father-in-law. When Judah finds out, he wants to execute her until he realizes he's the father. Then he knows "she is more righteous than I" (Gen 38:26). Tamar doesn't just want a son in the line of Judah. She wants her children to share the inheritance of Abraham, Isaac, and Jacob, which they do: Tamar ends up in the line of Jesus, the son of Judah, the son of David (Matt 1:3).

Ruth is a Moabitess, a child of Lot's incest with his older daughter. At times, she looks just like her ancestress. Like Lot's daughter, she approaches a man at night—a man who has been drinking, a man who addresses her as "daughter." She lies at his feet (perhaps a euphemism for genitals) and asks Boaz to spread his wing over her (Ruth 3:6-13), a marital gesture. Typical Moabitess, we might think, but Boaz sees the truth: "you are a woman of excellence" (Ruth 3:11), a model of the excellent wife (Prov 31:10-31). She's bold to the edge of scandal in order to become a new Eve, mother of the head-crushing Last Adam (Matt 1:5).

Tamar and Ruth are types of Israel, the Bride of Yahweh. They are brash Eves, like the beloved of the Song of Songs. The Bride of the Song is not a "nice" girl. She doesn't remain within the polite confines of social convention. Her lover comes to her door, oiled with perfume, and the aroma drives her mad (SoS 3:6). Her escapades in the streets (SoS 3:1-5; 5:2-8) look suspiciously similar to Lady Folly's. She is untamed in her passion for her Bridegroom. And she's black, burned by the sun (SoS 1:5-6). Solomon's beloved has the untamed, exotic beauty of a black goddess. In this, Solomon resembles Moses, who has a "Cushite" bride (Num 12:1-2). The Bride of the Song is like Mary Magdalene, a scandalous woman (Luke 8:2) who desperately seeks Jesus and finds Him in a garden (John 20:1-18). She is an Eve who mistakes Jesus for Adam the gardener.

We catch a whiff of allegory: Yahweh doesn't choose His Bride from the domesticated, prim ladies of the city. Yahweh chooses a black, beautiful, unpredictable Bride to make her Queen at His right hand. Yahweh chooses the shrew.

Miracle Mothers

Eve is the mother of all living, the first woman who gives birth to the first sons and daughters (Gen 4). All other mothers in Scripture are new Eves.

Like Eve, they labor under the curse: "I will greatly multiply your pain in childbirth; in pain you will bring forth children" (Gen 3:16). Rachel is an Eve who dies in tears as she gives birth to Benjamin (Gen 35:5-8). Scripture is about the triumph of life over death, and women are the heart of the story. Many new Eves have trouble *getting* pregnant. By Adam's sin, death is unleashed on the world (Rom 5:12-21), and death takes hold of the source of life, the mother's womb. But where death abounds, life abounds all the more.

Yahweh promises Abraham seed like the stars of heaven and the sand of the seashore, along with a land of milk and honey. When Abraham first enters the land, there's a famine (Gen 12:10).

Even before that, we learn that Sarah is barren (Gen 11:30). Death blocks Yahweh's promises and Abraham's Adamic destiny. If Abraham is to be a new Adam, Sarah needs to become a new Eve. Yahweh the Creator can overcome dead wombs. He makes the wilderness blossom like a rose. He opens Sarah's womb and gives her a son (Gen 21:1-7). The Abrahamic promise comes to fruition when Sarah becomes fruitful. The vocation of humanity moves forward through a new Adam *and* a new Eve.

Another generation, another dead womb, Rebekah, the wife of Isaac, is barren too. Again, the Lord brings life from the grave. He secures the destiny of Abraham's children (Gen 25:21). Jacob is surrounded by fertile women—Leah, Leah's maid Zilpah, and Rachel's maid Bilhah. Rachel herself is barren (Gen 29:31) until Yahweh remembers her, removes her reproach, and gives her a son, Joseph (Gen 30:22-24), the son who will preserve his whole family alive by giving out grain in Egypt. Yahweh's plan for Israel continues because Rebekah and Rachel, like Sarah, become new Eves.

At crucial junctures in Israel's history, Yahweh repeats the wonder. The Hebrew women in Egypt aren't barren, but their children are stillborn by Egyptian policy. If Israel is to be redeemed from slavery, if they are to inherit the land Yahweh promised Abraham, He will have to bring life from dead wombs. He raises Moses from the waters of death, the Nile where Hebrew boys had been drowned (Exod 1–2). By their cunning, Moses' mother, Jochebed, and his sister, Miriam, cheat death to deliver the future deliverer. The Nile's death waters become the womb of a new world.

At the end of the period of the judges, Yahweh again intervenes—twice—to open closed wombs. Manoah's wife is barren, a cursed Eve like Sarah (Judg 13:2). Throughout the annunciation scene, she is called "the woman" or "Manoah's wife" (Judg 13:2, 3, 6, etc.; *'ishshah*, "woman" or "wife," is used 14 times).

EVE

She is another Eve, "*the* woman," the original *'ishshah*. She bears Samson, one of the head-crushingest of Israel's heroes, whose name connotes "sunshine" because his advent is a new dawn for Israel.

At nearly the same time, pious, beleaguered Hannah visits the tabernacle at Shiloh. She not only bears the shame of barrenness but has to put up with the mockery of her husband Elkanah's second wife, Penninah. Hannah asks Yahweh to open her womb and give her a son and promises to dedicate her child to Yahweh's service. She gets what she asks, a son whose very name means "God hears": Samuel (1 Sam 1; *shama'* + *'el*).

Samson and Samuel are Yahweh's one-two punch that KOs the Philistines. Together, they prepare the way for the coming of the kingdom and dynasty of David. Because "the woman" and Hannah become Eves, the whole nation of Israel moves from death to life. And behind "the woman" and Hannah, readers whose senses are on the alert will glimpse the shadow of Eve, mother of all living.

Sarah, Rebekah, Rachel, Manoah's wife, Hannah—all are portraits of Yahweh's corporate Bride, Zion. Zion, too, is a barren woman. When Yahweh's Servant comes, Zion begins to stir, and sound is the first sign that she's alive. "Shout for joy, O barren one, you who have borne no child; break forth into joyful shouting and cry aloud, you who have not travailed" (Isa 54:1). Jerusalem's homes and streets have been empty, silent as graves. But when the Servant bears away sin and prolongs His life, Zion breaks into song.

She sings because she's no longer alone. The barren woman has become a joyful mother of children. Yahweh tells Zion to embiggen her tent because her house will once again be filled with children, her courts once again teem with worshipers. Zion is raised from death to become mother of the living (Isa 54:1-3).

Mothers sometimes consume children rather than give

them life. When the curses of the covenant intensify, when cities are besieged into famine, even the most refined and delicate woman eats her offspring (Deut 28:54-56; Lam 2:20). This is not a gruesome symbol. It actually happens. During Aram's siege of Samaria, two women ask King Jehoram of Israel to settle a dispute about eating their babies (2 Kgs 6:24-31). It's a macabre reprise of Solomon's judgment of the prostitutes (1 Kgs 2:16-28).

Zion becomes a cannibal mother, eating her children's flesh and drinking their blood through economic abuses and injustices (Isa 10:1-4; Lam 4:10; Rev 17:7). Zion imitates Sheol, who, like the barren woman, never says, "Enough" (Prov 30:16). Zion becomes the anti-Eve, anti-mother of the dead. If old Zion can turn cannibal, so can new Zion, the church, which has been known to chew up and gobble down her best children.

Warrior Brides

Eve is the mother of the Seed who crushes the serpent's head. Mothers and sisters shout with savage joy when that happens. Miriam leads the women of Israel in song and dance, boasting that Yahweh hurled Pharaoh and his horses into the sea (Exod 15:1-21). The women of Israel praise David after he bashes and removes Goliath's head (1 Sam 18:1-9). Heaven praises the Lamb after He and the martyrs overthrow Babylon (Rev 19:1-6).

Women don't just praise the head-crushers. The Bible records redemptive history, the story of sin and salvation. It's a story of maturation as Adam grows up to the Last Adam, from glory to glory. It's also a story of God's holy war against Satan. It may come as a surprise that the women of Scripture are as crucial to the holy war as they are to God's victory over death. A surprising number of Eves don't *praise* head-crushers; they *are* head-crushers.

Deborah and Barak lead the armies of Israel against Jabin, king of Canaan, and his general, Sisera. Despite having 900 chariots (Judg 4:12-13), Sisera gets routed from the field because Yahweh fights for Israel. Escaping on foot, he passes by the tent of Jael (wife of Heber, the Kenite), who offers to hide him. She gives him milk and covers him with a blanket. As soon as Sisera falls asleep, she pulls out a mallet and drives the tent peg through his temple (Judg 4:17-22). Like the woman at Thebez, Jael is Eve and her Seed rolled into one, a warrior bride who herself bashes the serpent's head and is celebrated in Deborah's song (Judg 5).

Abimelech, son of Gideon, kills all seventy of his brothers on a single stone (probably as sacrifices) and declares himself king (Judg 9:1-6). When Shechem rebels, Abimelech takes his revenge (Judg 9:22-45). He's a violent, vicious man. He has a mentor. "Abimelech" means "my father is king," and, sure enough, Gideon was a king in all but name. He assembles a harem (Judg 8:30) and makes an ephod that leads Israel into idolatry (Judg 8:22-27). Abimelech continues Gideon's trajectory toward standard-issue ancient kingship.

Until Abimelech meets his match. During a battle at Thebez, he gets too close to a tower, and a woman rolls a millstone off the top, which hurtles down to flatten Abimelech's head (Judg 9:50-57). Abimelech has all the military gear and soldiers, but a lone woman stops him with a tool for grinding grain. Like Jael's, this woman's weapons are household tools. You *can* do this at home.

While Judah is in exile, Haman plots to destroy the whole Jewish nation. Mordecai puts the Jews in peril because of his stubborn refusal to bow to Haman, which is similar to Queen Vashti's refusal to appear before King Ahasuerus. Fortunately, there's an Eve at the court: Esther, a female savior, who appeals to the king, tricks Haman into revealing his duplicity, and wins the day for Israel. By the end of Esther, Mordecai is elevated to the place vacated by Haman (Est 10). An Adam takes the throne because of the courage and heroism of an Eve.

Jesus is the child who plays by the adder's hole (Isa 11:8).

He is the Seed who tramples the serpent and drives him from heaven (Rev 12:5-12). But the victory belongs to the Last Adam's Bride as well as to Adam. Jesus tells His disciples they will toy with snakes (Mark 16:18; cf. Acts 28:3), and Paul tells the Romans they will crush Satan underfoot shortly (Rom 16:20). In all these passages, a Spiritual reader recognizes the new Eve, the church, who joins her Bridegroom in overthrowing Satan.

Jael points to another dimension of this typology. The Bible's warrior women use *deception*. Sarah and Abraham deceive Pharaoh and Abimelech by telling them half-truths about their relationship (Gen 20:8-13). Tamar deceives Judah to trick him into giving her an heir and a share in the line of Abraham (Gen 38). The Hebrew midwives lie to Pharaoh to protect infant boys (Exod 1:15-22), and God is so pleased with them that He gives them households. Michal, daughter of Saul and wife of David, lies to her father to protect the future king (1 Sam 19:11-17).

Rahab is one of the most complex Eve figures in the Bible. A prostitute, she seems primed to be a false Bride, a figure of idolatrous Israel. Instead, she proves faithful. When Joshua's spies show up at her inn/brothel, she confesses her fear of the God of Israel. Forty years after the exodus, Jericho is still panicked about Yahweh (Josh 2:8-11). Rahab wants to be on Yahweh's side, and she's willing to renounce the king of Jericho to join the winning team. She protects the spies, hides them on her roof, and then sends the local soldiers off in the other direction on a wild good chase (Josh 2:1-7).

"Shame, *shame* on Rahab," tut the commentators. "She's right to protect the spies, but she shouldn't have *lied*." The Bible never breathes a word of criticism. Instead, Rahab's whole house is rescued; she marries into Israel and, like Tamar and Ruth, wins a place in the genealogy of Jesus (Matt 1:5). She's a model woman of faith (Heb 11:31), comparable to Abraham as an example of the harmony of faith and works (Jas 2:14-26). Rahab's story shows what faith *is*: public, active loyalty to the God of Israel.

Our senses should be attuned enough to catch a whiff of Eve. The first Eve was deceived by the serpent and ate the forbidden fruit. New Eves reverse the process and deceive serpents and Satans. It's the symmetry of Yahweh's justice. Eye for eye, tooth for tooth, life for life, lie for lie, a lie leading to death overcome by a lie leading to life.

The Bible's Adams are often strongmen and warriors. Abraham fights a war. Moses leads Israel in battle, and so do Joshua and Gideon and Samson and Samuel and David. But the best warrior-Adams are the ones who learn to use the tactics of the warrior Brides. One of the remarkable things about David is how frequently he uses deception. He's the greatest Adamic warrior because he fights like an Eve.

Marian Church

Mary is the new Eve in person. She gathers all the great women of Scripture into herself. She doesn't listen to a serpent but receives Gabriel's unexpected news with a simple, "Behold the bondslave of the Lord" and "May it be unto me according to your word" (Luke 1:26-38). The first Eve is promised a Seed to crush the serpent's head, but Mary gives birth to that Savior.

Though not barren, Mary is a new Sarah, a new Rebekah, Rachel, Hannah. She's a virgin, yet the Spirit overshadows her to give her *the* miracle Son. Her Son is the true Isaac, born of Spirit, not flesh—a new Jacob, the true Israel. Jesus, Son of Mary, is a riddling warrior like Samson, a prophet like Samuel.

Like Hannah, Mary sees her son's birth as the catalyst for revolution in Israel. The Lord will throw down the high and lift those in the dust. He fills the hungry and sends the rich away empty. He remembers and fulfills His promises to Abraham (Luke 1:46-55; cf. 1 Sam 2:1-11). Israel comes alive again because of Mary's miracle Child.

Mary receives the same accolade as Jael—most blessed among women (Judg 5:24; Luke 1:42)—because she gives birth to the Seed of the Woman who crushes the serpent's head once and for all. She is the greatest of the warrior women.

As the Last Eve, the Bride of the Last Adam, the church is corporate Mary. Barren though we may be, the Spirit makes us fruitful. The church is called to be virginally pure yet also a mother. The church is a warrior Bride, called to join her Husband in battle, called to take up millstones and hammers to crush heads and slay giants. With our senses trained by Scripture, we can grasp the church as Mary, laboring until Jesus is born among us (Gal 4:19).

Queen of Heaven

Paul makes it clear that Adam and Eve are figures for Christ and the church. That's the theological basis for his exhortation to husbands and wives (Eph 5:22-33). The "great mystery" is that marriage discloses Christ and the church. Paul expounds the Christ-church relation by quoting Genesis 2: The two shall be one flesh.

To say the church is Eve is to say the church lives in intimate communion with her Husband, submitting to His authority, living as one flesh in one Spirit with Him. The church is the Bride of the Song of Songs. Aroused by the aroma of her Lover, she is relentless in pursuing His company. That should be *you*.

But Eve isn't merely a figure of intimate communion. To say that the church is the *eschatos* Eve is to say the church is a helper suitable to the *eschatos* Adam. The Last Adam is the King who rules all things and fills all things. The church is the Queen at His right hand to share His throne, majesty, and authority. We are Miriam; we are the women of Jerusalem, dancing and singing at the victory of *our* Moses, *our* David.

The Last Adam is the Priest who serves in the house of His Father. The church is the Levitical priestess who assists Adam in His priestly work. The Last Adam is the liturgical Leader; the church is the Bride who speaks in response. The Last Adam is the Prophet with access to the council of God, the Prophet who brings the indictment against the world and who petitions the Father. The Last Eve is the prophetess, a new Miriam and Huldah, who hears, reports, and intercedes.

The church is Eve *glorified*. At the beginning of the Song of Songs, the Bride is despised—an outcast oppressed by her brothers, blackened by the sun. By the end of the Song, she has become not just a beauty but a cosmic beauty: "Who is this that grows like the dawn, as beautiful as the full moon, as pure as the sun, as awesome as an army with banners?" (SoS 6:10). By the end of the Song, she receives the name "Shulammite," a feminine version of the name "Solomon" (SoS 6:13). Through the course of the Song, she is conformed to her lover. She becomes the feminine version of the King. The Song is about the "Solomonification" of the Bride. *That's* you too.

That's the promise of the gospel. We are made one-flesh with the Last Adam by His Spirit and so are conformed to Him. We become the Bridal version of Jesus, the feminine form of the new humanity. Our perfume is the aroma of the Last Adam, the aroma of Christ—to the world, an aroma of life and death (2 Cor 2:14). Humanity began as a man, Adam. When the progress from glory to glory is complete, when the new humanity reaches full maturity, we will be Eve, Bridal Jerusalem. For the woman is the glory of the man.

That's a wonder. But our senses should be alert to a still greater wonder.

Before Eve's creation, Adam is simply "Adam." He receives his name from his origin: Taken from the *'adamah*, he is *'adam*.

Adam is of earth, earthy. He speaks for the first time when he sees Eve. He names himself, but he doesn't name himself "Adam." He doesn't call the woman "Adamah" because she was taken from "Adam." Rather, he calls her "woman," *'ishsheh*, because she was taken from him, the man, the *'ish*. Both words are derived from the Hebrew word *'esh*, "fire." Once Eve appears, Adam is no longer simply a man of earth. He's a man of fire. He becomes a burning altar. After he sees Eve, he's lit.

Guys know what this is like. We're lit for life by the woman we love. Jesus knows it too. Jesus is the Last Adam, the church the Last Eve. Like the first Adam, the Last is "lit" by His Bride.

Here's the final wonder: The Son has bathed in the glory of the Spirit from everlasting to everlasting. *And yet* He is *glorified* and enflamed by the beauty of His Bride. He is intoxicated with her perfumes as she arises as a sweet-savor. Jesus has entered into glory. But like the first Adam, He won't enter into the fullness of His glory until His Bride is with Him—a spotless Bride without blemish or wrinkle, a heavenly Bride who is also a city and a temple, a mother and a Queen. Jesus will not have all His glory until He has you and me in glory with Him.

5   EDEN

His fruit was sweet to my taste.
Song of Songs 2:3

The lights dim. The first shot is a dusty, windswept road. Tumbleweed rolls and bounces across the screen.

Quick: What kind of movie is this? When the camera pans around to show a settlement, what kind of buildings are there? If the camera pans to the landscape, what will it look like? How do you know?

The camera saunters into a small town. It moves toward a doorway with two swinging half-doors. Music drifts from within. What kind of business is this? What kind of music do you expect? What other sounds will you hear? What will you see when the camera pushes inside? How will people be dressed? What will they be doing? *How do you know*?

Suppose you hear one of Beethoven's late quartets. Are you surprised? Why? Suppose the camera moves inside to reveal a set of elegantly dressed people watching a Shakespeare play. Will *that* surprise you? Why?

Suppose someone walks out the door. How will he be dressed?

THEOPOLITAN READING

What sort of footwear will he have? If the doors swing open and U.S. Supreme Court Justice Ruth Bader Ginsburg or Pope Emeritus Benedict XVI or the Dude from *The Big Lebowski* walks out, will you laugh? Why?

Another film, another opening scene: A cloudy night with only a glimmer of moonlight. A bolt of lightning flashes and illuminates a house. What kind of house is it? How do you know? What if you see Pope Benedict or the Dude peering from a window? Will you laugh?

We don't think twice about guessing what's going to happen in a movie. We've become accustomed to the conventions of filmmaking. We know the house illumined by the lightning flash will be a Victorian mansion, probably rundown, likely with a scary turret. Directors of short films depend on this. They only have thirty minutes and need to set our expectations very quickly. Fortunately, they only need five seconds of film. Like a sidewalk caricaturist, the director sets a scene with a few strokes of his pen. He can do that because we know the formulas: Dusty road + tumbleweed = Western. Stormy night + old house = thriller.

If you don't know these tricks, you'll be lost. It'll take you a few minutes to get your bearings. Finally, it dawns on you: "Ah, yes. This is the Old West. That is the sheriff. Oh, and that brassy lady in the frilly dress runs a brothel." A practiced movie-watcher has his senses trained. He knows all this instantly.

If you haven't developed a taste for the conventions, you won't notice when they're being violated. Ruth Bader Ginsburg comes out the saloon doors, and you shrug, "Hmm. Interesting." It's only jarring or humorous to viewers expecting someone else— John Wayne, Clint Eastwood, Brad Pitt, or some other square-jawed tough with a badge. If you don't know the conventions, you don't just miss a nuance. You miss *everything*. If you don't know what fits, you won't sense that Justice Ginsburg doesn't fit. You won't know there *is* a joke, and you certainly won't *get* the joke.

EDEN

The premise of this book is that Scripture has its own conventions, rooted in the early chapters of Genesis. Adam is the conventional male figure, and his vocation and actions set the pattern for the men who come after—Noah, Abraham, Jacob, Moses, Aaron, the judges, Samuel, David, Solomon, Elijah, Isaiah, and on and on till the advent of the Last Adam.

If you don't know Adam thoroughly, you won't spot the meaningful variations on the theme. You won't recognize Noah as an improved Adam. You won't realize that Yahweh's promise to make Abraham "fruitful" is a promise to fulfill Adam's vocation in Abraham's seed. You won't see the Adamic features of Aaron the priest. You won't sense that Solomon has what Adam doesn't, namely, knowledge of good and evil. You won't recognize the prophets as Adams who have reached a stage of maturity that Adam never reached.

Most importantly, if you misconstrue how Jesus is the Last Adam, you'll miss the heart of the gospel. You might think Jesus comes to whisk us from earth to heaven. In fact, the gospel presents Jesus as the Last Adam, who has fulfilled the human vocation and is now fulfilling it on earth, by His Spirit, through the church. If your palate isn't trained to savor the Adams of the Bible, you won't have any good sense of who *you* are: a priest, king, and prophet, co-member of a community of priests, kings, and prophets joined to the great Priest, King, and Prophet.

Eve is the main female character, paradigm for the women of the Bible. As mother of the living, she sets the pattern for the Bible's miracle mothers—for Sarah, Rebekah, Rachel, Hannah, and the wife of Manoah. As sinner, she lurks behind the seductresses of Scripture. As mother of the serpent-crushing Seed, she's the model for the warrior women. Eve is deceived by the serpent, but other Eves—the Hebrew midwives, Rahab, Michal—gain victory *by* deception.

Spiritual readers sense Eve's presence in all her myriad

transformations and variations. Like a sommelier, a Spiritual reader tastes the hints of Eve in the story of Mary and the history of the church. Though there's an element of play in Spiritual reading, it's not an aesthetic or literary diversion. We discern the conventions of Eve so we can grasp the story of Scripture, which is the story of each of us and the story of the world.

The Bible has conventional, recurring characters. It also has conventional *scenes*: city, wilderness, temple, field, vineyard. If you want to learn to read well, you need to familiarize yourself with the conventions—the typical settings that recur throughout the Bible. Like all biblical themes, these conventional scenes all have their roots in the original scene, the garden of Eden.

I have sometimes given students a "pop culture" survey to test their knowledge of movies, music, and TV. They do scarily well. Some remember advertising jingles and silly sitcoms from *my* childhood. Then I give them a Bible trivia quiz, asking them to identify the daughters of Zelophehad or give the weight of Goliath's armor or identify Jeremiah's birthplace. On that test, they typically do—I put it delicately—*less* well.

My punch line is this: Earlier generations of Christian students and intellectuals treated the Bible as their "pop culture." Without concordances, much less search engines, they had the whole Bible at their fingertips. I imagine Origen riffing away on snatches of the Bible, as today's teens and twenty-somethings can fill hours with movie quotes or pop song lyrics. And my exhortation to them and to you is this: The Bible needs to become *at least* as second nature as pop culture.

Garden, Vineyard, Temple, City

The Bible sometimes refers directly to the garden of Eden. When Yahweh restores Zion, He makes it like Eden (Isa 51:3). The prince of Tyre is Adam or the serpent in Eden (Ezek 28:13).

Pharaoh is such an immense, majestic tree that all the trees of Eden are jealous (Ezek 31:9), but Pharaoh will be cut down just like lesser trees (Ezek 31:18). After Yahweh brings Israel from exile, He gives His people new hearts and puts His Spirit in them, so the wasteland again becomes an Eden (Ezek 36:35). Joel prophesies of a locust plague that turns an Edenic land into a burnt-over district (Joel 2:3).

Scripture refers to "gardens." Even without the name "Eden," the allusion is clear. Lot chooses to live near Sodom because at the time it's "well-watered everywhere . . . like the garden of the Lord" (Gen 13:10). Moses reminds Israel they're entering a land watered from heaven, where they don't have to use a foot pump to irrigate their vegetable gardens (Deut 11:10). Giving water from heaven, Yahweh Himself ensures that Canaan remains a garden-land.

Jehu pursues King Ahaziah of Judah through the "garden" gate of Samaria (2 Kgs 9:27), a hint that Ahaziah is a fallen Adam driven from Eden. Later, the garrison of Jerusalem flees through the same garden gate as Babylonians flood into the city (2 Kgs 25:4). Godlike Ahasuerus throws a banquet in his palace garden (Est 1:5) and later pronounces judgment against Haman, a Satan, near a garden (Est 7:7-8).

If Judah keeps the true fast and true Sabbath, they will flourish like a garden (Isa 58:11), as righteousness and justice spring up like plants (Isa 61:11). Jesus prays in a garden as He begins to re-open the gate of Eden (John 18:1). After His resurrection, Mary Magdalene mistakes Him for the gardener (John 20:15), a mistake that reveals the truth: Jesus is the Last Adam.

A vineyard is a special form of garden. Noah plants a vineyard after the flood (Gen 9:20). Yahweh uproots Israel from Egypt and plants her as a vineyard, which He hopes will produce wine to delight God and man (Judg 9:13; Isa 5:1-7). When it produces bad fruit, He tears down the wall and leaves it to be trampled by unclean beasts (Psa 80:8-13). Israel is to be a new Eden.

She becomes a wilderness.

Orchards are Edens (SoS 4:13; 6:11). So are groves of trees (Josh 24:13) and forests (Isa 29:17; 32:15-19). During Solomon's reign, every family in Judah has its own vine and fig tree (1 Kgs 4:25). Canaan is Edenland, each man an Adam, every woman a fruitful vine (Psa 128:3), every plot a little outpost of Eden.

Gardens, vineyards, orchards, and groves don't occur naturally. They're planted, cared for, and cultivated. Yahweh sets the example by planting the first garden. As His images, human beings plant and tend gardens too.

Cultivated gardens can mature into something more solid, permanent, and glorious. When Yahweh renews the land, He also causes "cities to be inhabited, and the waste places to be rebuilt" (Ezek 36:33-35). Zechariah envisions the ideal future as a city with peaceful streets filled with laughing children as the elderly look on (Zech 8:1-5). John's final vision is of a city that looks a lot like Eden—tasty fruit, tress of life, water, purity (Rev 21:22—22:5).

These aren't visions of a *return* to Eden. They're visions of a *built-up* Eden, an urban Eden, the world subdued so as to become a garden-city. Even the most pastoral prophecies of Isaiah envision a new-and-improved Eden. Lions lying with lambs, bears and oxen grazing together: This is a world *after* Adam's task is complete, when humanity has tamed the beasts (Isa 11:1-10). This isn't the world of the first Adam but of the Last.

Revelation adds another dimension (Rev 21:1—22:5). New Jerusalem isn't a garden or simply a city. It's a garden-city and also a *temple*. It's a house for God and the Lamb, a house for His images, the saints who populate the city.

Genesis 1 and 2 already anticipate the temple of new Jerusalem. Creation is a temple-building project.[4] The tabernacle and

---

[4] See *Theopolitan Liturgy*, 4-14.

temple are world-models, and, reasoning backwards, we conclude the world is a temple. God builds a cosmic house in three zones, and the tabernacle and temple have three zones. After forming and filling, God places His image in His house, a sign of His presence. At the end of the creation account, Yahweh is enthroned in rest in His cosmic house.

The garden is also a temple. Every other sanctuary in the Bible is modeled after the garden. Each sanctuary is a well-watered place. Every one is a place of festivity. Yahweh speaks with Adam in the garden, and each sanctuary is a dwelling place for Yahweh, centered on Yahweh's Word. After the fall, cherubim guard the garden (Gen 3:21), and every sanctuary in the Bible is adorned with figures of cherubim and guarded by human cherubim, the priests and Levites (Exod 26:18-22; 1 Kgs 6:23-35).

World, garden, and temple overlap and interpenetrate. If we read of a garden, we should also taste the hints of a fruitful land and the temple and the world itself as potential garden. When we examine the details of the tabernacle or temple, our senses need to be trained to spot elements of a glorified garden. We need to learn to read at several levels at once: The natural (garden, land), the liturgical (temple), and the civic (city) all mirror each other. We can fold in the Bridal imagery from chapter 4 because cities and temples and gardens are feminine spaces.

Let me give you a for-instance. Is the Song of Songs a love poem (marital)? Is it the king's paean to the beauty of his land (natural)? Is it about the temple (liturgical) or the city (civic)? The answer is yes. In some portions, Solomon the king celebrates features of the land and the glory of his people. At other times, the erotic dimension is at the forefront. Throughout, Solomon draws on the imagery of the temple. As a poem, the Song is all about all of them.

"Our couch is luxuriant! The beams of our house are cedar, our rafters, cypresses," says the Bride near the outset of the

THEOPOLITAN READING

Song (SoS 1:16-17). She's describing the trysting place where lovers meet. But the description alludes to the temple. The temple is paneled with cedar of Lebanon (1 Kgs 6:9-20); Solomon builds a house of the forest of Lebanon, and his throne hall is paneled with cedar (1 Kgs 7:7). Cypress, too, is one of the materials of the temple (1 Kgs 5:8, 10). The word translated as "luxuriant" means "green" (*ra'anan*), and the temple is a "forest" or "grove," an interior space conceived as a natural place (cf. Psa 52:8; 92:14). Though man-made, it's a green world where people flee for refuge and renewal. There, Israel finds apples to taste, the fruit of her beloved (SoS 2:3, 5).

There are competing "green spaces" throughout Israel, idolatrous shrines under every "green tree" (Deut 12:2; 1 Kgs 14:23; 16:4; 2 Kgs 17:10), where Israel plays the harlot (Jer 2:20; 3:6, 13). All the while, the green space of the temple is there, Yahweh's own cedar-and-cypress grove where He promises to make love to His Bride on a green couch.

The poem refuses to be pinned down. It relentlessly mixes the natural, the liturgical, the marital, and the civic. Spiritual readers develop the refined taste to savor and distinguish all the flavors.

None of this is mere "imagery." The overlapping garden-temple-land-city allusions point to the vocation of mankind and the purpose of human history. Adam has a task in the garden and a task in the world. The two tasks are connected because the garden-temple sets the pattern for the cosmic temple. The garden is the template (pun initially unnoticed), the little taste of heaven that anticipates what Adam will achieve on earth. Adam's task in the world is to glorify the world until it's a *civic* Eden and a dwelling of God.

This is Israel's task as well. Yahweh gives them a good land of vineyards and orchards and olive trees they didn't plant, a land of cities they did not build (Deut 6:10-15). They build the garden-sanctuary in the land and are called to transform the

EDEN

whole land into a temple. As a priestly people, they guard the garden-land. As a royal people, they extend the garden into the corners of the land.

Man's vocation and history's meaning are woven into the literary fabric of Scripture. History is the gardenification of creation, the Edenification of the planet, the new-Jerusalemification of the cosmos, the temple-ization of the original cosmic temple, the heavenization of earth.

Wilderness

Adam is created to subdue and rule the earth until the cosmic temple becomes a garden-temple. Instead, he disobeys and turns the world into a wasteland.

The desert is everything the garden is not. In the wilderness, there is no water (Exod 15:22; 1 Kgs 17:1-7; Psa 63:1). Instead of fruitful trees, there are brambles and cacti. There's no food, and after forty years the only food available doesn't taste so great (Num 21:5).

There are animals, but they're wild and uncooperative toward human beings—jackals (Psa 44:19; Isa 35:7), ostriches (Isa 43:20), wild oxen (Num 23:22), and donkeys (Job 6:5). There are predators and scavengers—lions (1 Sam 17:34-37; Jer 4:7), leopards (Jer 5:6), wolves (Jer 5:6), vultures (Isa 18:6), bears (2 Kgs 2:24), tree snakes, and hawks (Isa 34:13-15). The desert isn't a place for human beings, and those unfortunate enough to be cast out into the wilderness don't thrive or exercise dominion. The desert is the un-garden.

Cities are civic expansions of the garden, but cities, too, can be reduced to wilderness. Zion becomes a wilderness, Jerusalem a desolation (Isa 64:10). Isaiah's mission lasts until Yahweh the Judge empties out the cities of Judah (Isa 6:11). Israel's enemies leave Jerusalem in ruins (Psa 79:1) and break the city's walls and fortifications (Psa 89:39-40). Yahweh threatens to demolish

Moab (Isa 15) and Damascus (Isa 17). He turns fortress cities into ruinous heaps (Isa 37:26). Wild Gentiles trample the vineyard.

Sometimes Israel's own leaders do the trampling. Yahweh tells Jeremiah that He's just completing what Israel's shepherds started. Before Yahweh judges Judah, the leaders have already turned the garden city into a wilderness and made Yahweh's "pleasant field a desolate wilderness" (Jer 12:7-13). Under Yahweh's judgment, the city is reduced to the *tohu* and *bohu* that preceded Yahweh's forming and filling (Isa 34:11).

You can tell a city has become a wilderness when you find hyenas in the towers and jackals wandering through palaces (Isa 13:22; Jer 10:22; 49:33). Instead of vineyards, olive groves, or fig trees, a wilderness city is full of thorns and briers (Isa 34:13). You know a city is on its way to being undone when it's unpeopled (Jer 2:15; 4:7; 9:11).

Temples can become desolate too. If Israel doesn't keep covenant, Yahweh threatens to rip apart His own house until not one stone is left on another (1 Kgs 9:8). Psalm 74 laments the destruction of the temple by axe-wielding pagans (Psa 74:1-11), who chop down the temple as if it were a "forest of trees" (Psa 74:5). Nebuchadnezzar burns Solomon's temple, but Israel had made it abominable long before. Ultimately, Yahweh tears down what He builds, cursing Israel for her infidelity. That warning is central to Jesus' ministry: Not one stone will be left on another because the house is filled with desolating abominations (Matt 24:1-2, 15).

The good news is that Yahweh is in the habit of bringing life from death. He is, after all, the Creator. Once there was nothing, then something. Once there was a watery wasteland in utter darkness. Then the Spirit and Word illumined, formed, and filled the world of glory we inhabit. If the Lord can bring something from nothing, *everything* from *tohu w-bohu*, He can make the wilderness fruitful, rebuild cities, raise up His ruined house, and re-ascend to His throne. When our senses are trained by Scripture, we'll see graveyards as wombs, rubble as material for a new temple, dry bones as a future army.

This story of death and resurrection recurs again and again in Scripture and history. Yahweh brings Israel from Egypt, then leads them into a howling waste—without water or food, without fields to plant or harvest, without shelter. Many Israelites look longingly back to slavery in Egypt, which from a hazy distance looks a little like Eden. Then Yahweh brings water from the Rock (Exod 17:1-6; Num 20:1-13), enough water to sustain two million people. He rains bread from heaven (Exod 16:1-7) and quail for the grumblers in the mixed multitude (Exod 16:8-21). He protects Israel from her enemies and leads her through the wilderness in a pillar of cloud and fire.

When the prophets look back to the exodus, they see Yahweh turning the wasteland into a garden. He turns the arid wilderness into pools of water (Psa 107:35; Isa 41:18). He makes the desert rejoice and blossom like a rose. Carmel, Lebanon, and Sharon are among the most fertile areas of ancient Israel, but Isaiah says the Lord will give their glory to the desert (Isa 35:1-3). When He pours out the Spirit who hovered over the emptiness at creation, He turns a barren land into a fertile field and the field into a forest (Isa 32:15-16). The vineyard returns, and Yahweh comes to taste the wine.

The prophets who look back to the exodus expect Yahweh to do it again. The God who delivered Israel from Egypt will deliver them from the Philistines. He brought them from Egyptian bondage, and He will lead them back from Babylon. He gave them a land full of gardens, orchards, groves, vineyards, and cities. Those may be in ruins, but He will bring it all back again. Edenland will be restored. Where there has been nothing, Yahweh will spread a banquet to dazzle Israel's eyes and delight Israel's tongue.

THEOPOLITAN READING

Yahweh gives hope to Israel's desertified cities. Barren Zion will be filled with children (Isa 54:1). Disfigured, ruined Jerusalem longs to be made new. When Yahweh returns, He glorifies His Bride. She will no longer be tossed like a ship on a turbulent sea but set firm on a solid foundation of gems and precious stones (Isa 54:11-12). Zion will be adorned as a Bride in her sparkling gown. She'll become a crystal city with foundation, gates, and walls of rubies and sapphires. She will be set in the firmament, a sapphire pavement under her feet and a sun shining within her (Isa 54:11; 60:1-3). And Zion the jeweled city will be *utterly* safe (Isa 54:13-17).

Zion becomes a harlot. The city once full of justice becomes a haven for murderers. Her rulers are rebels and thieves, lovers of bribes. Instead of defending orphans and widows, mother Zion devours them. Innocent blood is on her hands. When the Servant has come, Zion will again become a "city of righteousness, a faithful city" (Isa 1:26). Because of the Servant, the Righteous One, she will be established in righteousness, and Yahweh will silence all the blasphemy against Himself and all the slanders against Zion. By building His crystal city, He justifies His Bride: "This is the heritage of the servants of the Lord, and their vindication is from Me, declares the Lord" (Isa 54:17).

This repeated melody comes to a crescendo with Jesus. He announces the end of the temple and city. Jerusalem will be desolated. He also promises a new temple. He raises the temple of His body in three days, and fifty days later He pours His Spirit to fill the new temple of the church. Jerusalem has become Babel, mother of harlots (Rev 17). But a new Bride comes, formed and adorned in heaven, descending to earth (Rev 21—22). The New Testament is also a story of desolation and renewal, of desertification that gives way to gardenification.

Let me sum all this up with a chart:

	Natural	**Liturgical**	**Civic**	**Marital**
Positive	Garden/land	Temple	City	Bride
Negative	Wilderness	Ruined temple	Empty city	Harlot

The Bible doesn't sharply distinguish between these zones of life. A healthy city can be pictured as a garden or a faithful bride. An idolatrous temple can be described as a wilderness or a harlot. The Bible has an intricate, built-in pattern of imagery, rooted in creation, rooted in the opening chapters of Genesis with Adam, Eve, and Eden.

I remind you again: This isn't literary ornamentation. Jerusalem really does have a temple with orchards and gardens. Jerusalem really is destroyed. Nebuchadnezzar really burns the temple. I imagine some wild animals actually prowl the ruined buildings and unkept yards. It all *actually happens*. And it happens again in the first century when the Romans assume Babylon's role to flatten Jerusalem.

The restoration is real too. After seventy years of exile, Cyrus sends the Jews back to the land. Joshua and Zerubbabel re-erect the temple (Ezra 6:13-16), and Nehemiah rebuilds the city walls. Isaiah's prophecies come to pass. Cyrus gives them gold and other treasure, cypress and cedar, to restore the temple (Isa 60:6, 9, 13). Kings minister to Israel, and foreigners help rebuild their walls (Isa 60:10). Yahweh really re-plants what He uprooted. Jesus builds a new temple, a new *kind* of temple of living stones, from the debris of the old.

Even prophecies that don't seem literal have a literal force. The parallel lines at the end of Isaiah 60:5 compare "abundance of the sea" to the "wealth of nations." The background, as we saw in chapter 2, is the consistent use of the sea as an image of the Gentile world (cf. Jer 6:22-23). Isaiah promises that when the Jews

THEOPOLITAN READING

return to the land, they'll go fishing. Gentiles will rise from the sea to worship Yahweh and bring their sunken treasures to Zion to adorn and maintain the house of Yahweh. Israel will taste and eat of the delicacies of the Gentile sea.

Christians often spiritualize prophesies like this. Yahweh's restoration of Zion pictures regeneration. God "vindicating" Zion portrays justification by grace through faith. Building up Zion represents going to heaven when we die. Many believe the Old Testament was oriented to the earth, while the New Testament directs us to heaven. The Old is about bodies; the New is about souls. The Old is about external things; the New moves inside.

None of that fits the Bible. Spiritualized reading isn't Spiritual reading. They're nearly opposites. From beginning to end, the Bible is about *this* world. It's a book about God by being a book about God-and-the-world. It's a book about heaven, but only insofar as it's about heaven-and-earth. Guided by the Spirit, Spiritual readers learn to discern the inner workings of the world and its history.

Imagine you live in ancient Israel and hear Isaiah or Jeremiah or Ezekiel. What do you think they're talking about? It's clear they're describing what's happening to Jerusalem, the capital city of the Davidic dynasty. They prophesy its destruction and reconstruction. They describe a series of actual events under the literal-figures of wilderness and garden, of desertification and Edenification. They predict and recount political events— the destruction and restoration of a *polis*, a city. A Theopolitan reading of Scripture won't miss the *polis*.

The prophets clarify the biblical meaning of "salvation." It doesn't just have to do with forgiveness and communion with God. Salvation is the restoration and glorification of broken creation. Saved people are restored to God's favor. But they're also restored in their relations with one another and with the world. Saved people form the body of Christ, knit together as a new humanity by the Spirit. Saved people become new Adams and Eves equipped by the Spirit to be fruitful, multiply, fill, subdue, and rule the earth.

New Testament passages that talk about a ruined temple and city are just as this-worldly as the Old. Jesus prophesies the destruction of Jerusalem and the Second Temple in A.D. 70 (Matt 24; Mark 13; Luke 21). The city John sees is about a real polity, the church, the heavenly city that is already being built on earth.[5]

In the Bible, salvation is *this*-worldly. It takes a communal, political form in the church. It takes the form of a communion of real men and women and children who serve their neighbors, stand for justice, pray and praise, hear the Word, and taste the bread and wine of the Lord's table. Where you see *that*, you see salvation taking form in the here and the now.

Traces of Eden

Let's go back to those movie scenes. How much of a Western film do you need to see before you know it's a Western? Not much. A few seconds of footage and you're in. If you want to thicken the atmosphere and reach for an Oscar, you can start with an endless scene at a railway station, silent except for the unremitting drip-drip of rain water from the roof onto a gunslinger's hat.[6]

How much does a biblical writer need to evoke Eden or the anti-Eden of the wilderness? Zion or the rubble of ruined Zion? The temple or the charred remnants of the temple? If we're biblically literate—as attuned to the Bible as we are to the movies—the answer should be, "Not much." A few strokes of the pen, a few seconds of film, and we know exactly where we are.

---

[5] See *Theopolitan Vision*, ch. 1.

[6] I'm describing the opening scene of *Once Upon a Time in the West*.

What's in Eden? Eden is on a mountain (Ezek 28:13-14). There are trees and two special trees at the center, with fruit (Gen 2:9). A river flows from the land of Eden and through the garden, splitting into four rivers (Gen 2:10-14). There are animals, which Adam names (Gen 2:18-20), and people, eventually a man and a woman. Soon enough, there's a serpent at the tree, tempting Eve (Gen 3:1). And after Adam sins, there are cherubim at the gate, guarding the way of return (Gen 3:24).

Sometimes, we find all or most of these features together. The temple is built on a high place, Mount Moriah (2 Chr 3:1). It's possible there were groves surrounding the temple, but we know for sure the temple is lined with cedar and the floor covered with cypress. The two bronze pillars at the door are designed like giant lilies (1 Kgs 7:15-22). There's no gold in Eden, though there was gold downstream in the land of Havilah (Gen 2:11). In the temple, the gold has been transported up to Eden to adorn the sanctuary. There's the stylized almond tree of the lampstand. There's no fruit in the temple, but there's bread and strong drink and wine for libations—plant products transformed by labor into food.

The temple is a well-watered place like the garden of God (Gen 13:10). In the court is a great bronze sea set on the backs of twelve bronze oxen, and ten water stands form a "stream" of water flowing from God's house out to the world (1 Kgs 7:23-39). There are animals in the temple courts—oxen, sheep, goats, and birds turned to smoke as a soothing aroma before Yahweh (Lev 1—7). There is an Adam, the priest, and his "helpers," the Levites. Cherubim are carved into the cedar walls of the temple, and two gold cherubim form Yahweh's throne in the inner sanctuary (1 Kgs 6:23-32).

Cities also share many of the features of Eden. Ancient cities are often on mountains, and they need to have water sources. There are animals, trees, food, and people. Ancient kings boast of their elaborate gardens and parks (cf. Eccl 2), and even the sleekest modern cities have their Central Parks, their Hyde Parks, their Yoyogi Parks.

But the Bible doesn't always provide full-scale portraits of Edenic scenes. It doesn't have to. Like the filmmaker, the biblical writers trust us to pick up a whole scene from one or two hints.

The Bible is full of high places that touch the floor of heaven: Sinai, Ebal and Gerazim, Pisgah, Zion, Moriah, and Olivet, the "upper room" where Jesus has a new covenant feast with the Twelve. Each is a recapitulation of Eden. And so are all the mountain-like things in the Bible. Altars are mountains. Towers are mountains. Temples are mountains. Pillars are mountains; some even have Edenic flora on their capitols. The biblical writers don't have to put up a blinking sign to announce, "This is a new Eden!" A brief reference to a mountain is enough for the attentive reader to know where he is.

Isaac's servant meets Rebekah at a well (Gen 24:10-21). Jacob first meets Rachel at a well and rolls away the large stone at the well's mouth (Gen 29:1-12). Moses fights off the surly shepherds who pester the women at the well in Midian so that Jethro's daughters, including his future wife Zipporah, can water their flocks (Exod 2:15-22). On his way to be anointed as king, Saul meets women going to draw water; soon, Saul will be "in-lawed" to Israel (1 Sam 9:11-14). In Samaria, Jesus meets a woman at a well and discusses her marital history (John 4).

A man, a woman, and water. Where are we? We're not in a Western or a Gothic horror film. We're in Eden, and Isaac, Jacob, Moses, Saul, and Jesus are all Adams finding their Eves in a well-watered place.

Or try this: a tree, full of green leaves, fruit hanging, near a river. It's Psalm 1, where the Psalmist uses the image of the tree to describe the righteous man who chews over Torah day and night. Psalm 1 places us in Eden: The righteous man is a tree of life and establishes a little Eden around him. So does the righteous woman, an Eve, who is a fruitful vine at the corners of her house (Psa 128:3). The Psalmist doesn't need to sketch the whole picture to make his point. He assumes we know our way around. He trusts us: When we see a tree and water, our senses should leap back, and forward, to the tree of life.

The negative environments don't need to be spelled out in detail either. "You will be like an oak whose leaf fades away," says Isaiah 1:30. You don't need any more to infer what kind of setting you're in: The tree is dying. Its leaves are brown. Perhaps there's no water. We're somewhere on the path of desertification. The following line seals it: "as a garden that has no water" (Isa 1:30b).

A filmmaker doesn't need a widescreen shot to evoke a ruined city. A coyote scrabbling at a garbage can will do it—or an unweeded yard, or peeling paint on the siding of a once-luxurious home, or a crumbling stone wall. Biblical writers evoke scenes of civic ruin with passing references to jackals and wild animals in houses (e.g., Isa 13:22), to desert animals or plants in what should be a civic garden. Jerusalem's water supply is poisoned by wickedness (Jer 6:7). When we see that, we sense we're in anti-Zion. Wild beasts and birds of prey inhabit the city, feasting on corpses (Jer 7:33). We're in a fallen Jerusalem. Yahweh lets loose adders and serpents in the city (Jer 8:17). We're back in Genesis 3.

And the biblical writers don't have to paint a detailed canvas to speak of the restoration of Eden, of the city, of the temple. A change in plant and animal life is enough to evoke the renewal of creation. Because of the sins of Judah, the land is filled with thorns and briars (Isa 32:12-13), and emptied, a haunt for wild donkeys (Isa 32:14). It will not remain so forever. The wilderness will not remain wilderness; the briars and thorns will not remain briars and thorns. When the Spirit comes, everything turns around; everything changes (Isa 32:15). The wilderness will become fertile, and the fertile field will explode into a forest. Where injustice and oppression reign, righteousness will spring up, and the fruit of righteousness will be peace, security, quietness, and confidence. Instead of wild donkeys, the land will be full of herds of cattle and domestic beasts of burden.

Conclusion

Jesus is Adam. He fulfills the vocation of Adam to fill, subdue, and rule the earth. The church is Eve, a helper suitable to the Last Adam, tasked to join Jesus in filling, subduing, and ruling creation. Eden is the down payment of a glorified world. Adam is created to transform the world into an Edenic temple-city. He fails and instead turns Eden into a wasteland. The Last Adam reverses the process, so the earth is renewed, the city rebuilt, the temple purified. Jesus accomplishes all that and then sends us out to finish up the task.

Spiritual reading trains our senses to see this cast and this plot over and over within Scripture, in never-exact repetitions. Spiritual reading trains us to see this cast and this plot in *our* lives and *our* world. Barbarians breach the walls of Rome to loot the city, and Augustine knows he's living through a biblical story. He knows the city's end isn't *the* end, so he writes a visionary book that prepares the church for the world after the world's end. English settlers land on the shores of North America and see before them a wilderness that needs to be Edenified. (Tragically, they view Native Americans as Canaanites.) A pandemic rages across the globe during the spring of 2020, a pestilence like those predicted by Jeremiah and the prophets. Cities go silent, work stops, and weddings are canceled. We sense that a world is ending. But we face it with hope because we know God always makes new Edens spring up from the wastelands.

THEOPOLITAN READING

Theopolitan reading is about more than reading. Theopolitan reading is inextricably linked to the Theopolitan vision of the church's mission and the Theopolitan reading of history. Spiritual reading is necessarily political reading, ecclesial reading, missional reading. Jesus is the Last Adam. We the church are the Bride, the new Eve, at His right hand. As we read the Bible as a story of Eden given, Eden lost, Eden regained, Eden glorified, we're reading about *ourselves, our* mission, the mission of the Last Adam and His Bride.

EPILOGUE

The glory of kings is to search out a matter.
Proverbs 25:2

So you've finished the book, almost. Perhaps you've gotten excited about new possibilities for reading Scripture. With me as your mentor and model, you're ready to dive in and notice things in Scripture you hadn't noticed before. I hope so.

Perhaps you're a pastor beginning to prepare your next sermon, a Sunday school teacher working on a lesson, or a plumber, nurse, designer, electrical contractor, landscaper, carpenter, or mom who wants to enrich your personal Bible reading and your family worship. You're ready to start. What do you do?

It's been my mantra from the preface on: What you do first is find a guide and stick with him or her. You need teachers, mentors, other people. You need to apprentice yourself to a master reader. Sometimes, the master will be the author of a book, rather than a friend or pastor. It's better, though, if you can find a live mentor so your reading can mature in its natural setting of communion and conversation.

It's been another mantra: Your senses are trained when

THEOPOLITAN READING

you follow Jesus the Teacher, who is also Jesus the Host of the banquet. If you want to become a king who searches out the secrets of Scripture, join a church where the worship is drenched with Scripture, a church that communes each week at the Lord's table, a church faithful in evangelism, discipleship, service. Spiritual reading happens in Spirit-filled churches.

I'm not being coy. Those things are essential.

Still. You want to know what to do when you sit down tomorrow for your morning Bible reading. You flip the pages and start reading. You want some rules or guidelines, at least some suggestions. What should you notice? What should you pay attention to? Your senses are on the alert: but for *what?* There are four corners of the earth, four winds of heaven, four corners of the altar, and four Gospels. Therefore, pay attention to four things:

- What the passage *says*. Who does what to whom? Where is this event taking place and when? What happened just before this, and what happens after? What was said in the previous chapter, and what is said in the next chapter? Pay attention to the letter. *Always* follow the letter, and let the Bible set the terms for your reading. Pay attention to how the writer says what he says, the turns of phrase and allusion, the metaphors and similes. How does this verb or noun, this metaphor or allusion, throw your mind to another section of Scripture? How are the two passages similar and different?
- What the passage says about *Jesus*. Everything in Scripture says something about Jesus. Everything in the *universe* discloses something about Jesus, the Creator Word in whom all things cohere. How does the passage send you back to Adam and Eve in Eden or to one of the many other Adams and Eves and Edens? How does it project you forward to Jesus and the church in the world? How does the *way* things are said point you to Adam or Jesus? What does the passage teach you to *believe* about God, Jesus, humanity, the world? Pay attention to what the Bible says about *faith*.

EPILOGUE

- What the passage says about *you* in Jesus. Everything in Scripture is about Jesus. You are "in Christ Jesus." So everything in Scripture is about *you*. The whole church is "in Christ," the Body and Bride of Christ, one flesh with Him. If the whole Bible is about Jesus, it's also about the *church*. How does the passage reach back to Eve or the many Eves of Scripture? How does it launch you ahead to think about the Last Eve, the new Jerusalem? What does the passage tell you about yourself as a member of the church, part of the Bride of the Last Adam? How does it teach you to understand your experience, the condition of the church and the world, in the light of Christ? What does it teach you to *do*? Pay attention to what the Bible teaches about *love*.
- What the passage says about *your future* in Jesus. Everything in Scripture is about Jesus. Jesus came and will come. He is the Alpha *and* the Omega. Everything in Scripture teaches about Jesus and His future. And you are in Him, so everything in Scripture tells you something about *your* future. Every passage says something about the future of the church and the world. Ask how the passage takes you back to Eden, to gardens, vineyards, garden-cities, and temples. How does it reach forward to new Jerusalem? What does it teach you to *hope* for?

As you read, the Spirit and Word will work to conform you—your heart, your mind, your will, your imagination—to the living Lord Jesus. Scripture is the food that nourishes you in faith, hope, and love. As you read, you become a gloss on Jesus the Word, a living epistle of God's love and justice, a king or a queen whose senses are trained to discern good and evil.

You're ready now. *Tolle lege.* Take up, read. And *labete phagete.* Take, eat.

FOR FURTHER READING

Jordan, James B. *Creation in Six Days: A Defense of the Traditional Reading of Genesis One.* Moscow, ID: Canon Press, 1999.

Jordan, James B. *From Bread to Wine: Creation, Worship, and Christian Maturity.* Monroe, LA: Athanasius Press, 2020.

Jordan, James B. *The Handwriting on the Wall: A Commentary on the Book of Daniel.* Atlanta: American Vision, 2007.

Jordan, James B. *Judges: God's War Against Humanism.* Eugene, OR: Wipf & Stock, 1999.

Jordan, James B. *Primeval Saints: Studies in the Patriarchs of Genesis.* Moscow, ID: Canon Press, 2002.

Jordan, James B. *Through New Eyes: Developing a Biblical View of the World.* Eugene, OR: Wipf & Stock, 1999.

Jordan, James B. *The Vindication of Jesus Christ: A Brief Reader's Guide to Revelation.* Monroe, LA: Athanasius Press, 2009.

Leithart, Peter J. *Deep Exegesis: The Mystery of Reading Scripture.* Waco, TX: Baylor University Press, 2009.

Leithart, Peter J. *Delivered from the Elements of the World: Atonement, Justification, Mission.* Downers Grove, IL: IVP, 2016.

Leithart, Peter J. *1 & 2 Chronicles*. Grand Rapids: Brazos Press, 2019.

Leithart, Peter J. *1 & 2 Kings*. Grand Rapids: Brazos Press, 2006.

Leithart, Peter J. *The Four: A Survey of the Gospels*. Moscow, ID: Canon Press, 2010.

Leithart, Peter J. *From Behind the Veil: The Epistles of John Through New Eyes*. Moscow, ID: Canon Press, 2009.

Leithart, Peter J. *The Gospel of Matthew Through New Eyes*, 2 volumes. Monroe, LA: Athanasius Press, 2018-2019.

Leithart, Peter J. *A House for My Name: A Survey of the Old Testament*. Moscow, ID: Canon Press, 2000.

Leithart, Peter J. *The Promise of His Appearing: An Exposition of Second Peter*. Moscow, ID: Canon Press, 2004.

Leithart, Peter J. *Revelation*, 2 volumes. London: T&T Clark, 2018.

Leithart, Peter J. *A Son to Me: An Exposition of 1 & 2 Samuel*. Moscow, ID: Canon Press, 2003.

Leithart, Peter J. *The Ten Commandments: A Guide to the Perfect Law of Liberty*. Bellingham, WA: Lexham Press, 2020.

Meyers, Jeffery J. *A Table in the Mist: Ecclesiastes Through New Eyes*. Monroe, LA: Athanasius Press, 2007.

Roberts, Alastair J. and Andrew Wilson. *Echoes of Exodus: Tracing Themes of Redemption Through Scripture*. Wheaton, IL: Crossway, 2018.

Sumpter, Toby. *A Son for Glory: Job Through New Eyes*. Monroe, LA: Athanasius Press, 2012.

www.ingramcontent.com/pod-product-compliance
Lightning Source LLC
Chambersburg PA
CBHW031120080526
44587CB00011B/1046